Beginner's Chess Course

Enno Heyken

Sterling Publishing Co., Inc.
New York

Photos by Peter Pinzer
Translated by Annette Englander
Edited by Claire Bazinet

Library of Congress Cataloging-in-Publication Data Available

10 9 8 7 6 5 4 3 2 1

Published by Sterling Publishing Company, Inc.
387 Park Avenue South, New York, N.Y. 10016
Original German language edition, *Schach für Einsteiger,*
published by Falken-Verlag GmbH
© 1996 by Falken-Verlag GmbH, 65527 Niedernhausen/Ts.
English translation © 1997 by Sterling Publishing Co., Inc.
Distributed in Canada by Sterling Publishing
^{c}/o Canadian Manda Group, One Atlantic Avenue, Suite 105
Toronto, Ontario, Canada M6K 3E7
Distributed in Great Britain and Europe by Cassell PLC
Wellington House, 125 Strand, London WC2R 0BB, England
Distributed in Australia by Capricorn Link (Australia) Pty Ltd.
P.O. Box 6651, Baulkham Hills, Business Centre, NSW 2153, Australia
Printed in the United States of America

Sterling ISBN 0-8069-9969-1

CONTENTS

History of Chess and the World Champions

Egocentrics, geniuses, artists, and "cold-war warriors"

Backgammon, checkers, and other board games can be challenging. Many card games, such as bridge, require a great deal of mental effort. Nevertheless, for centuries, no game has been a match for chess.

Only those who are unfamiliar with chess will be surprised at that statement. Anyone who knows the rules and can enjoy the tremendous challenges of the game can well understand its very special fascination.

At any time, you can replay a chess game originally played by such chess superstars as Garry Kasparov or Anatoly Karpov. This allows you to appreciate it in much the same way that a music enthusiast enjoys the complexities of a Beethoven symphony or the ingenious arrangement of a piece by Pink Floyd.

Chess teaches us to think logically, to defend ourselves carefully, to accept defeats, to learn from mistakes, and to develop and trust intuition. Even though chess is a strictly logical game, intuition plays a very decisive role in the success of all chess players.

Of course, the game itself is indeed interesting. But the "chess scene," especially the professional championships, can be just as fascinating.

Chess is a very old game. It is believed that it was invented about 500 A.D. in India. Over the years, the rules have changed drastically, but the rules we know today have remained essentially unchanged since the beginning of the nineteenth century.

Morphy – The First Superstar of Chess

By the sixteenth and seventeenth centuries, some clergymen, such as Ruy López of Spain, were so fascinated by the game that they studied it intensively and wrote books about it. López was particularly interested in opening moves. The Ruy López Opening, also known as the Spanish Opening, is one of the best known of all the standard openings.

However, it wasn't until 1857 that chess had its first unofficial world champion, Paul Morphy from New Orleans. Unlike other players of his time, Morphy knew how to use his pieces as a unit and how to organize his attacks on the basis of solid positions. Morphy's combinations were often so elegant that, even today, people enjoy replaying many of his games. His most famous one, which he played while seated in a box at the opera during a performance of *The Barber of Seville*, is the first example game of this book.

Morphy was more than successful; he was the prototype of a hero: young, good-looking, ingenious, and he was an American. In 1858, at the age of twenty-one, Morphy defeated almost every leading master in Europe. In 1859, he returned to America to an enthusiastic reception. Soon afterward, Morphy retired from chess. He had proven that he was far superior to any of the other players of his time, and championships no longer

presented him with a real challenge. Viewed historically, his retirement as an unbeaten champion was certainly a coup. As is the case with some more modern world champions, part of the myth surrounding Morphy is that he was invincible.

Steinitz – A World Champion of Defense

After Wilhelm Steinitz won a match against Adolf Anderssen (in 1866), he replaced Morphy as the world champion.

Steinitz regarded chess in a new way. He was not interested in a "brutal" attack on the opponent's king. Instead, he preferred the art of defense and a strategic game against his opponent's weak spots. At times, his ideas were somewhat eccentric. For example, in some of his opening variations he quickly moved his king into the center of the board. Normally, chess players would consider such moves as positive proof of mental derangement. But Steinitz had dis-

covered that, in certain circumstances, the king can actually be a strong figure in the opening. In other games, Steinitz moved all his pieces back to the starting position because he was convinced of the strength of that position. These new ideas led to frequent altercations with his contemporaries. At the end of his career, he was defeated by a younger player.

Steinitz died in poverty because he lived before the era of huge purses for chess championships. According to some sources, at the end of his life he was more and more irrational. The story goes that he finally challenged God to a chess match, and he was willing to give God a one-pawn advantage.

Psychology and Philosophy – Lasker Sets New Standards

The Lasker–Steinitz match, played in 1894, was the first official world championship. From then on, chess had regular world championship matches.

Emanuel Lasker, who was twenty-five years old at the time, easily won the championship. He retained the title for twenty-seven years—quite an achievement. Lasker was a thinker who was interested in philosophy and had discussed it with Einstein. Lasker felt that, like life, chess is a psychic battle. For that reason, logical considerations were not always the determining factors for him. He tried to use psychology. He wanted to confuse the opponent, to explore and use his weaknesses. Instead of the best move, he often tried to find the most unpleasant move. Lasker brought a new dimension to chess. Because of his ideas, players began to realize that the game was more than pushing lifeless pieces of wood, that the game stands for the mental and spiritual struggle between two personalities.

Victory of Technique – The Endgame Artist Capablanca

The development of the game of chess continued. In 1921, José Raúl Capablanca, the pragmatic virtuoso, succeeded Lasker, the philosopher. The Cuban had an enviable talent. Although he had not dedicated himself to studying chess, he was a master player at the age of fourteen. Thus, he was the first "infant prodigy" of chess. Capablanca became famous for his technique. When he had a slight position advantage, he tried to exchange as many pieces as possible. Then he tried to win in the endgame, using precise maneuvering. When he was at the top of his game, he almost always succeeded with this strategy.

For Capablanca, the game often seemed easy. He moved very fast, and he lost only a few games in his entire chess career. He was the Mozart of chess. He knew instinctively what other people had to work years to learn. In addition, Capablanca was good-looking and had quite a few female admirers.

Return of Strength and Beauty to Chess – Alexander Alekhine

In 1927, Alexander Alekhine, known as the combination genius, succeeded Capablanca. That was fortunate, because some people thought that Capablanca's technique would continue to the point where the game of chess was only a parade leading to the endgame.

Alekhine returned glamour to the game. He used combinations, and he sacrificed with a beauty and precision unknown until then. He did this using positions in a more mature way than had been possible when Morphy was alive. Alekhine's games display an immense strength. He was a passionate fighter; and, when he lost a game, he took out his frustrations by heavy drinking, sometimes ending up smashing glasses and even the furniture in his hotel room.

In 1935, Alekhine lost the title for a short time to Max Euwe, a Dutch professor of mathematics. Euwe was an excellent chess strategist and he wrote books on chess that are worthwhile reading even today. In 1937, Euwe granted Alekhine a return match. Alekhine humiliated Euwe with a score of 10 to 4.

Alekhine died in 1946, still the reigning world champion. Because of World War II, he had not defended his title again.

World Champions for a World Revolution – The Era of Soviet Chess

From World War II into the eighties, politics dominated chess. The communist leaders of the Soviet Union realized that chess could become a symbol of the mental superiority of communism. They developed the skills of their best players with good trainers. They paid their players salaries, creating professional chess players (which, of course, they did not like to admit).

The success of the Soviet players proved that professionals would almost always win: In fact, with one exception, every world champion of the second half of the twentieth century was from the Soviet Union. However, most of these players didn't seem to consider themselves as representatives of communist intellectual culture. They simply wanted to play chess and to be as successful as possible.

Botvinnik – the Chess Scientist

The dominating figure from the end of World War II into the sixties was Mikhail Botvinnik. In 1948, he won the world championship after a series of matches involving the five best players of the time. With two interruptions, Botvinnik remained the world champion for fifteen years.

Botvinnik pursued the athletic and scientific character of the game much more professionally than his predecessors. He always arrived at competitions in excellent physical condition. He developed a number of opening systems which he analyzed like a scientific dissertation. Botvinnik had to work hard for his success; but, for him, the scientific element of the game constituted its special fascination.

In 1957, Vasily Smyslov was able to take Botvinnik's title away from him. Smyslov was an excellent strategist, but during the return match in 1958, Botvinnik used his excellent preparation to help defeat Smyslov and regain his crown.

World Champion of the Risk Game – "Chess Magician" Tal

In 1960, Mikhail Tal, an unusually ingenious attacking player, was able to beat Botvinnik. Opponents feared Mikhail Tal's daring, tactical intuition and his calculation. Some of his opponents even believed that Tal had hypnotized them. Rumors can easily lead to craziness in chess; thus, some opponents would wear dark sunglasses when they played against Tal. They felt that this protected them from the power of his eyes. That was, of course, nonsense. Mikhal Tal simply had a very unusual tactical talent, and he combined this with an extraordinary willingness to take risks. In some games, he even succeeded in making respected master players look like beginners. In regard to the world championship, though, the "magic" was over one year later —when Botvinnik defeated Tal in the return match.

Deep Concepts and Strange Moves – Tigran Petrosian

In 1963, Tigran Petrosian ended the unique career of Botvinnik as world champion. Judged by his style, Petrosian was perhaps the strangest world champion in the history of chess. His moves were often difficult to understand. Frequently they were not classical, and sometimes they were somewhat odd. He loved ponderous games in which both sides had to use tricky maneuvers to win. Usually, when Petrosian lost a piece, he had deliberately sacrificed it as part of a strategy to improve his position, not just to check the king.

All-Around Player and Gentleman – Boris Spassky

In 1969, Boris Spassky succeeded Petrosian as world champion of chess. Spassky was an all-around player, equally strong in almost all aspects of the game. His appearance on the chess scene was generally appreciated because he was a likable player and he showed good humor and a certain championlike distinction. Here was a world champion who was well suited for the beginning of the media era. But after winning the world championship, Spassky had no great desire to dedicate his life exclusively to chess. He only played in a few matches as world champion, and he was not quite as successful as you would expect a world champion to be. Besides his love of the game of chess, Spassky also had a love of the finer things in life. Thus, it is probably no coincidence that he lives today in France.

Showdown on the 64 Squares – Bobby Fischer and "The Championship of the Century"

In 1972, the time was ripe for the most fascinating figure of twentieth century chess, Robert James ("Bobby") Fischer from New York. By that time, Fischer had already won a fantastic series of tournament victories, crowned by his successes in the world championship matches in which Fischer crushed both Taimanov and Larsen, both by the amazing score of 6–0! But the world championship in 1972 became known as "The Championship of the Century," for different reasons. At the time, the Soviet Union and the United States were still fighting the cold war, and the two players seemed to represent the souls of their nations. One was a nonchalant, egocentric American who seemed like the embodiment of the individualistic American way of life. The other was a representative of the Soviet Union, supported by a host of officials and seconds.

Fischer did not disappoint the media. At first, he demanded financial rewards and threatened not to play if officials did not meet his demands. Then he shocked the organizers with more requirements. At one point, he insisted that the lighting be changed. At another, he insisted that the spectators were too close. After Fischer made what seemed to be a beginner's mistake, losing the first game in an absurd way, he did not even show up for the second game; he claimed that the cameras bothered him. The score was 2 to 0 in favor of Spassky.

It was then that a flood of telegrams arrived, reaching Fischer in his hotel room. Each one urged him to continue the competition and to win. Fischer did just that. He won the third, fourth, and sixth games, not letting go of his advantage to the end of the competition.

If Fischer had been simply an egocentric genius, he could not have electrified the world of chess so effectively. But Fischer was an unconditional lover of the game of chess. Whereas other tournament players were satisfied with a draw to secure a good tournament result, Fischer played every game for a victory. He always tried to take the initiative to put his opponent under pressure. He was a passionate player who enhanced the reputation of chess and professional chess players, even as he drove many tournament managers to despair with his eccentric requirements. Just as Paul Morphy had done, Fischer retired from chess after winning the world championship. In the nineties, he made a single-match comeback with another competition against Spassky. Fischer is a legend in his own lifetime.

The Esthetics of Perfection – Anatoly Karpov

The Karpov era began in 1975 after Bobby Fischer refused to defend his title. Karpov's style resembles that of Capablanca. He wins many games with his technique, especially his endgame. Combinations are relatively rare in his games. He plays very safely; and, thus, he only loses a few games. Many people accuse Karpov of playing boring chess. But take a look for yourself at example game 6 (pp. 106–112). The dreamlike serenity exhibited by Karpov in setting up his pieces has a special esthetic attraction. Many chess lovers prefer this to the "roaring cannon" style of other top players.

A New Era of the Attack Game – Garry Kasparov

Just as the chess world needed an Alekhine after Capablanca, so chess needed a Kasparov after Karpov. Kasparov won the chess crown in 1985 with a 5 to 3 victory over Karpov. He combines the essential virtues of the classical and the dynamic schools of chess. He is a hard worker with an excellent memory, and most of the time he is excellently prepared. He fights with all his energy for the initiative and wins many games with brilliant sacrifices. At the same time, he also understands how to treat simple positions.

More than Karpov, Kasparov is a man of the media. He loves to argue with other chess players and chess officials within the scope of press conferences. He did not hesitate in setting up a chess organization in direct competition to the world chess organization (FIDE). Suddenly, just as in boxing, several players were world champions at the same time. FIDE gave Karpov the world chess championship title; PCA gave Kasparov its championship title after a competition against Nigel Short of England. Nevertheless, at the end of the twentieth century, few people doubt that Kasparov is superior to Karpov, his opponent of many years. Kasparov succeeded in retaining his title through each of their last three duels, and he is the younger of the two.

Women Advancing in World Competitions

At the end of our discussion of the world chess championships, we want to talk about women in chess. Up until the latter part of this century, women hardly played a role in world chess. Girls rarely learned how to play; and, thus, they were a rarity at chess tournaments.

But in the eighties, three girls, the Polgar sisters, began their triumphal march into the world of chess. Their father had given them chess training when they were young. In fact, he raised them as child prodigies, especially the youngest sister, Judith, who won tournament victories at a very young age.

At fourteen, she was stronger than any player had ever been at that age, including Fischer and Kasparov. She has continued to develop, and today she is among the top players in the world. Many supporters of women's chess hope that one day she will be able to qualify for the world chess championship with men.

Without a doubt, there are women out there who have ability and have demonstrated good skills in chess, and we hope that the small number of women taking part in chess tournaments will increase rapidly in the years to come.

The Rules

Chess is a board game for two people. Even though you need years to reach championship levels, you can easily learn the rules in half an hour. To begin play, you only need a chessboard and a set of thirty-two chessmen (sixteen White and sixteen Black).

The Pieces and Their Starting Positions

Each chess game begins with all the chessmen (pieces and pawns) in the same starting positions. **1**

Each player has 8 pieces:

1 king	♔ ♚
1 queen	♕ ♛
2 rooks	♖ ♜
2 knights	♘ ♞
2 bishops	♗ ♝
and 8 pawns	♙ ♟

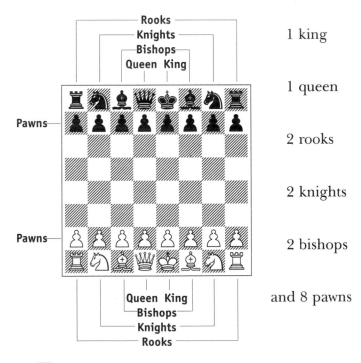

1 The basic starting position of every chess game.

	a	b	c	d	e	f	g	h	
8	a8	b8	c8	d8	e8	f8	g8	h8	8
7	a7	b7	c7	d7	e7	f7	g7	h7	7
6	a6	b6	c6	d6	e6	f6	g6	h6	6
5	a5	b5	c5	d5	e5	f5	g5	h5	5
4	a4	b4	c4	d4	e4	f4	g4	h4	4
3	a3	b3	c3	d3	e3	f3	g3	h3	3
2	a2	b2	c2	d2	e2	f2	g2	h2	2
1	a1	b1	c1	d1	e1	f1	g1	h1	1

2 The names of the squares on the chessboard.

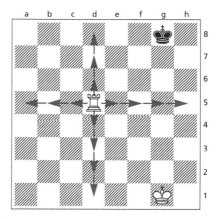

3 The White rook at d5 can move along any of these four paths.

Names of the Squares

Each board has sixty-four squares, and each square is identified with a letter and a number. The numbers (from **1** through **8**) identify the horizontal rows called ranks. The letters (**a** to **h**) identify the vertical columns called files. The diagram shows how to identify all of the squares. **2**

The White king starts each chess game on the square identified as **e1**. The Black queen starts on square **d8**.

Goal of the Game

White begins the game, making the opening move. After that, the two players alternate moves. Only one piece or pawn may occupy each square. A White man may never move to a square already occupied by another White man. However, both players can capture an opponent's man by moving onto a square occupied by that man. In that case, the opponent's man is removed from the board, and the capturing piece or pawn takes its place on the square. The goal of the game is to conquer, or checkmate, the opponent's king.

Movements of the Pieces

The Rook

The rook always moves and captures on a straight line along the ranks and files. He may move as many squares at a time as his player wants, but he never jumps.

Take a look at diagram 3. Here, nothing stands in the way of the rook's next move. On the next turn, he can move horizontally to squares

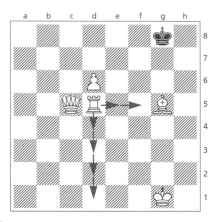

4 White's turn: The queen, bishop, and pawn are blocking the rook.

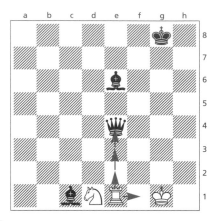

5 White's turn: The rook can capture the queen but not the bishop.

a5, b5, c5, e5, f5, g5, and h5. He can also move vertically to the squares d1, d2, d3, d4, d6, d7, and d8. **3**

The situation is different in diagram 4: Horizontally, the rook can only reach the squares e5 and f5. The squares c5 and g5 are already occupied by White pieces, and the squares a5, b5, and h5 are blocked since the rook cannot jump over other pieces.

Moving vertically, the rook can only reach the squares d1, d2, d3, and d4, because the pawn on d6 blocks all other possibilities. **4**

Diagram 5 illustrates how the rook captures. Notice the possible moves for the White rook on e1. He can move to the squares e2, e3, and f1. In addition, he can capture the queen on e4. On the other hand, he cannot capture the bishops on c1 or e6 because he may not jump over his own pieces or the opponent's pieces. **5**

The Bishop

The bishop always moves or captures diagonally. He can move as far as the end of the board, but he cannot jump. A bishop can never move to an opposite-colored square. Thus, each player has a bishop that moves only on the light squares and one that moves only on the dark squares.

Diagram 6 indicates the movement of the bishop. From the square e4, the bishop can move diagonally to the squares d5, c6, b7, a8, d3, c2, b1, f5, g6, h7, f3, g2, and h1. **6**

In diagram 7, the bishop's possibilities for moving are more limited. From c3, the White bishop can reach squares d4 and b4. However, he can also capture the Black knight on a5 or the rook on b2. Since the bishop may not jump, the only moves he has are the four possibilities just mentioned. **7**

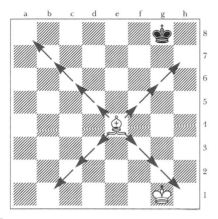

6 White's turn: The bishop moves diagonally, as far as the eye can see.

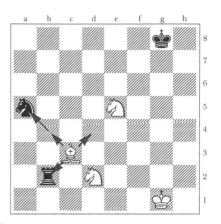

7 White's turn: The bishop can capture either the rook or the knight.

The Queen

The queen moves and captures horizontally, vertically, and diagonally. Thus, her moves are a combination of the rook's and the bishop's. She can move as far as she likes, but she cannot jump.

The queen is the most powerful piece in chess. Diagram 8 demonstrates the many possibilities a queen has. From **e5**, the queen can move vertically and horizontally, like the rook. In addition, she may move diagonally, like the bishop. **8**

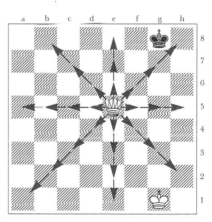

8 White's turn: Powerful queen combines moves of bishop and rook in one piece.

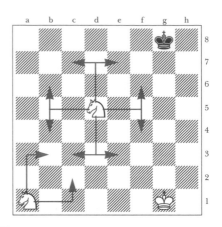

9 White's turn: His queen can capture the pieces on a7, b5, b8, and d5.

10 White's turn: Two straight, plus one to the side – the knight's jump.

Diagram 9 shows how the queen captures: The White queen on **b7** can move to **c7** and **b6** (as a rook could), as well as move to **a6**, **c6**, **a8**, and **c8** (as a bishop could). In addition, she can capture the Black men on **a7**, **b8**, and **b5** (as a rook could) or capture the Black knight on **d5** (as a bishop could). In this position, the White queen has no other possible moves. **9**

The Knight

The knight always moves or captures two squares straight and one square to the side. Thus, he can move in many different directions. In addition, the knight is the only chess piece that may jump over his own men or over his opponent's men. With each move he makes, a knight changes the color of the square he is on.

Now, take a look at diagram 10 and you'll understand how this complicated explanation actually works. You see two White knights and their possible moves. From his corner square, the knight on **a1** can only move to two other squares. His colleague on **d5** is in the center of the board. From there, he can move to eight squares. A knight never has more than eight possible moves. **10**

Diagram 11 shows how the two White knights capture and jump. The White knight on **a1** cannot go to **c2** because a White pawn is already occupying the square. But, he can capture the Black pawn on **b3** by jumping over the White pawns in front of him. The knight on **d5** has all eight moves available, as shown in diagram 10. If he moves to the squares **b6**, **e7**, or **e3**, he would capture Black pieces. **11**

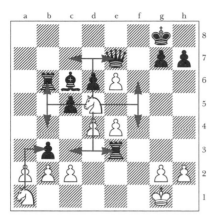

11 White's turn: No hurdle is too high, because the knight jumps!

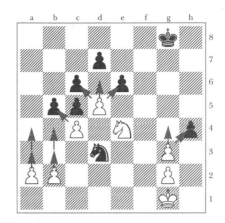

12 White's turn: Pawns move straight, but they capture diagonally.

The Pawn

A pawn moves forward one square at a time along a file. The only exception is that he may move forward two squares from his starting square.

But the pawn captures differently from the way he moves: The pawn captures one square diagonally forward. He never moves or captures backwards.

That sounds quite complicated, but look at diagram 12.

First, notice the pawn on **a2**. A pawn normally moves one square forward. That means the pawn can move forward to **a3**. Since he is still on his starting square, he may also choose to move to **a4**. His neighbor, the pawn on **b2**, can move to **b3** or to **b4**. Although the pawn on **g2** is still standing on his starting square, he cannot move because one of his own men is blocking him on **g3**; and, of course, he may not jump any pieces.

None of the other White pawns are on their starting squares anymore. Thus, they may only move forward one square at a time. A Black pawn blocks the White pawn on **c4**. The pawn on **c4** cannot capture the pawn on **c5** because pawns can only capture diagonally forward. Because pawns only move forward, the pawn on **c4** may not capture the knight on **d3**. The only possible move for the pawn on **c4** is to capture the pawn on **b5**.

The White pawn on **d5**, on the other hand, has more possibilities. He can move forward to **d6**, he can capture the Black pawn on **c6**, or he can capture the Black pawn on **e6**. The pawn on **g3** can move forward to **g4** or capture the Black pawn on **h4**. **12**

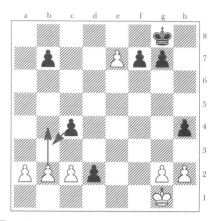

13 White's turn: If b2 pawn moves to b4, c4 pawn can capture *en passant*!

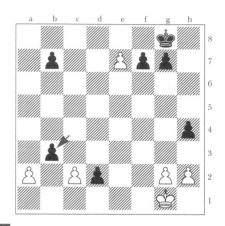

14 White's turn: Here is position after c4 pawn captures b4 *en passant*.

Diagram 13 shows another special rule involving pawns.

Special Rule 1: Capturing *en passant*
"*En passant*" is a French term that means "while passing by." In diagram 13, if White moves the pawn from **b2** to **b4**, then the Black pawn on **c4** can capture the pawn at **b4**. In capturing *en passant*, the pawn on **c4** moves from **c4** to **b3**, removing the White pawn on **b4**, creating the situation in diagram 14. **13** **14**

Capturing *en passant* is only possible immediately after an opponent's pawn has used one turn to move two squares forward from his starting square. Your own pawn must be standing next to the pawn after his move. You then capture his pawn as if the pawn had moved only one square forward. Remember, capturing *en passant* is possible only in the first

turn which follows your opponent's move. Have another look at diagram 14. The White pawn on **e7** has reached the seventh rank; the Black pawn on **d2** has reached the second rank.

Special Rule 2: Promotion
If it is White's turn to move, he can move his pawn from **e7** to **e8**.

Here, the pawn has reached the final square. White may now promote, or exchange, it for a piece. That means White may replace the pawn with any White piece, except the king. Promoting is always a very pleasant task, and in many cases you will exchange the pawn for a queen. Actually, you may find yourself replacing the pawn with a *second* queen. Although you may only have one king on the board, you may have as many other pieces as you can promote your pawns into. Here, White pro-

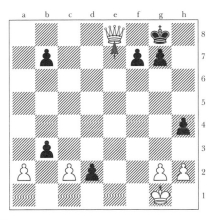

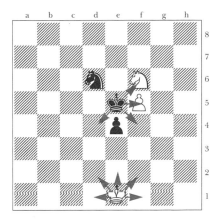

15 Black's turn: White has promoted the e-pawn to a queen.

16 The king can move one square in all directions.

motes his pawn to a queen, creating the position in diagram 15. **15**

Should you succeed in moving several pawns to the eighth rank (for Black, to the first rank), you can trade for any piece or pieces you want.

In case you do not have a second or even a third queen available, you can simply turn over a rook.

In diagram 14, when it is Black's turn, he can move his pawn from **d2** to **d1** and promote it to whatever piece he wants.

The General Rule

When pawns reach their promotion squares (White: eighth row; Black: first row), you immediately exchange them for the piece of your choice, except for the king.

The King

The king moves and captures one square in any direction, horizontally, vertically, or diagonally. The king may never move to a square which is threatened by an opponent's piece.

The king's movement is the simplest of all the chess pieces. It is illustrated in diagram 16. From **e1**, the White king can reach squares **d1**, **d2**, **e2**, **f1**, and **f2**. The Black king can move to **d4** and **f4**. He can also capture the White pawn on **f5** or the White knight on **f6**. The Black king may not move to **d5** or **e6** since the White knight and the White pawn threaten those squares. **16**

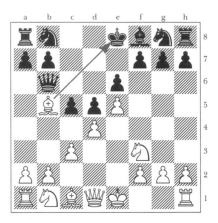

17 Black's turn: The bishop on b5 has the king in check.

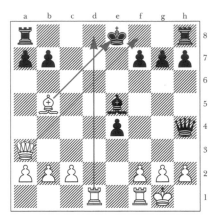

18 Black's turn: The king has no place to move – checkmate!

Check and Checkmate

When a piece or piece threatens to capture the adverse king in the next move, this is a "check."

You must get the king out of check at once. You can accomplish this by moving the king to a safe square, by capturing the attacker, or by blocking the line of attack (moving another man between the king and the attacking piece or pawn). If you cannot accomplish any of these, then the king is checkmated. Your opponent has defeated you, and the chess game is over.

In diagram 17, White has the Black king in check with his bishop on **b5** because he could capture the Black king in his next move. In this position, Black has three possible ways to react. **17**

❖ **flight of the king** – Black can escape the attack by moving his king from **e8** to **d8** or **e7**.

❖ **capture the attacker** – He can remove the threat by moving his queen from **b6** to **b5** and capturing the bishop.

❖ **block the attack line** – He can move the knight from **b8** to **c6** or to **d7**, blocking the line of attack. He can accomplish the same purpose by moving the queen from **b6** to **c6**. Any of these moves protects the king.

Black *must* move in such a way that White cannot capture his king on the next move. Therefore, Black must make one of the six moves outlined above.

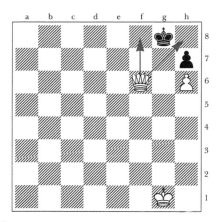

19 Black's turn: Stalemate! No check, but no legal move.

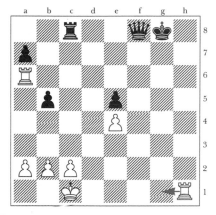

20 White's turn: Three repeats of same position and condition results in draw.

In diagram 18, the bishop on **b5** checks the king, but here, Black has no way to defend himself. **18**

❖ A Black pawn blocks a move to **f7**. Because the White queen is on **a3**, the king cannot move to **f8** or **e7**. The White rook threatens the **d8** square and the rook and bishop threaten the **d7** square.

❖ No Black man can capture the bishop on **b5**.

❖ No Black man can move between the bishop and the Black king.

In diagram 18, because Black has no way to escape from check, he is checkmated and loses the game.

Draw and Stalemate

When it is your turn, you can offer your opponent a draw and then make your move. If your opponent accepts, both of you receive half a point, and the game ends. Three other situations can result in a draw.

❖ When a player is not in check but cannot make a legal move, he is stalemated, and the game is a draw. Diagram 19 shows such a stalemate position. Of course, the position is only stalemate because it is Black's turn to move! If it were White's turn, he would move his queen from **f6** to **g7** and thus checkmate Black. **19**

❖ When a game reaches the same position three times with the same player on move, the game is a draw. **20**

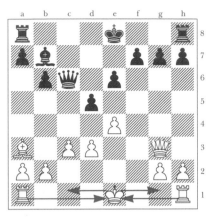

21 White's turn: Short and long castling.

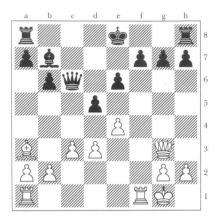

22 Black's turn: White has castled on the king's side—castling short (0 – 0).

In diagram 20, it is White's turn to move. Let's assume the game would take the following boring course: White moves his rook from **h1** to **g1** and checks the Black king. Black moves his king from **g8** to **h8**. The White rook moves from **g1** to **h1** and checks again. The Black king moves from **h8** to **g8**. Once more, White checks from **g1**, and Black moves his king from **g8** to **h8**. White's rook then checks on **h1**. Now, Black can end this tedious game by claiming a draw because when he moves his king from **h8** to **g8**, he will have reached the same position (the one in diagram 20) with the same player to move (White) for the third time. This is called a draw by "three-fold repetition."

❖ When neither side has moved a pawn or captured a piece in fifty moves, the game is a draw.

Castling

Diagram 21 shows a special move for the king and a rook. Called castling, it is an important game strategy. It allows you to remove the king from the center of the board, which can be a very dangerous spot, to a safer square on one side of the board. **21**

As shown in diagram 21, when it is White's turn, he may move his king from **e1** to **g1** and his rook from **h1** to **f1**. We call this move castling short because the move is on the short, or king's, side of the board. Diagram 22 shows the new position. The notation for this move is 0 – 0. **22**

Diagram 21 shows that White has another way to castle. He can move his king from **e1** to **c1** and his rook from **a1** to **d1**. He would then reach the position shown in diagram 23. Here, White has castled long. We call it long castling because it was on the

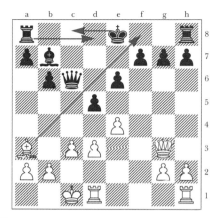

23 Black's turn: White has castled long (0 – 0 – 0).

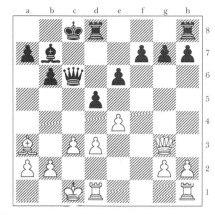

24 White's turn: The Black king did not cross over b8.

long, or queen's, side of the board. The long castle notation is 0 – 0 – 0. **23**

Rules for Castling

For castling short (on the short side), the White king moves from **e1** to **g1** (Black: from **e8** to **g8**). In the same move, the White rook moves from **h1** to **f1** (Black: from **h8** to **f8**).

For castling long, the White king moves from **e1** to **c1** (Black: **e8** to **c8**), and the White rook moves from **a1** to **d1** (Black: **a8** to **d8**).

It may sound complicated, but in practice, you simply move the rook next to the king and then jump the king over the rook. Once the king or the respective rook has moved, you may not castle, even if you move the piece back to its original position.

Each side may only castle once per game. You may not use castling to escape being in check. During castling,

the king may not pass through any squares which are under attack or controlled by the opponent. In addition, all the squares between the king and the rook must be empty.

For example, in diagram 23, Black may not castle short. On his trip, the king would move from **e8** to **g8**, crossing square **f8**. However, the bishop on **a3** is controlling that square. On the other hand, Black may castle long with the situation in diagram 23. Diagram 24 shows the position after Black's castling long. **23** **24**

Chess Notation and the Chess Clock

We write moves with the first letter for the piece, the starting position, a dash, and the ending position. For example, Nb1 - c3 indicates that the knight moves from the square **b1** to the square **c3**. When noting the move of a pawn, we only include the starting and ending squares. Thus, e2 - e4 stands for a pawn moving from **e2** to **e4**.

We show a capture with an **x** instead of a dash. For example, Nb1 x c3 tells us that a knight moved from **b1** to capture the opponent's man on square **c3**.

A plus sign at the end of a notation indicates that the move produced a check. The notation Bf1 - b5+ shows that the bishop moved from **f1** to **b5** and put the opponent's king in check. To repeat, 0 – 0 indicates castling short, and 0 – 0 – 0 indicates castling long.

When several moves are written consecutively, White's move always stands on the left and Black's move on the right. For example:

1. d2 - d4   d7 - d5

A good move is indicated with an exclamation mark (!) and a brilliant move with two exclamation marks (!!). Similarly, a bad move receives a question mark (?) and a bad mistake, also called a blunder by chess players, receives two question marks (??).

In this book, in order to distinguish normal moves from variations and threats, normal moves appear in regular type, while variations are underlined, and threats are written in *italic*.

The Chess Clock

In serious chess games, players write their moves on a score sheet. A clock controls the amount of time permitted for a game. Actually, two clocks are used. Each player stops his clock when he has completed his move. This automatically starts the opponent's clock.

The amount of time permitted depends on the form of the competition. In normal games, each player has a total of between three and four hours per game. On the other hand, "lightning chess" is played with only five minutes' time per player.

If a player has used up all the time allotted to him and the game is not yet over, the player loses, no matter how good his board position might be.

Test 1: The Rules

Exercise 1

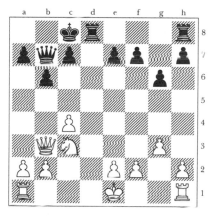

1 White's turn: Which pieces can move to square d3?

It is White's turn to move. Which of his men may he move to square **d3**?

Exercise 2

2 White's turn: Is 0 - 0 possible? Is 0 - 0 - 0 possible?

The king on **e1** and the rooks at **a1** and **h1** have not yet moved. Can White castle short in this move? Can he castle long?

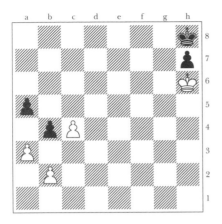   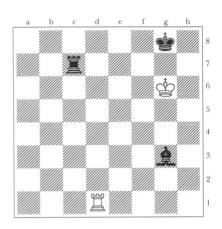

3 **Black's turn: What can Black move?**   **4** **White's turn: Checkmate in one move using rook and king.**

In White's last turn, he moved his pawn from **c2** to **c4**. What are Black's possibilities now?

It is White's turn to move, and he only has his king and a rook left. Nevertheless, White can checkmate the opposing king in one move. What is that move?

Exercise 5	Exercise 6

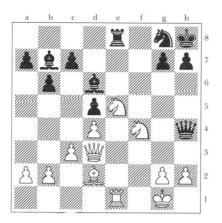

5 White's turn: Where can the two White knights go?

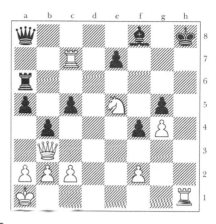

6 Black's turn: What defensive possibilities does Black have?

The Black king is trapped by his own men and has nowhere to move. What are the total number of possible moves for the two White knights in the diagram? What are they? Which move will checkmate the opponent?

White's rook on **h1** has the Black king in check. How many possibilities does Black have to get out of check? What are they? Which produces the best results?

27

The Value of the Pieces

Often in chess, players exchange pieces using the phrase "If you capture my knight, then I capture your knight." But what happens when you have an opportunity to exchange a knight for a bishop or a bishop for a rook? In order to decide whether or not to exchange pieces, you need an approximate idea of the value of the individual pieces. For that, we have to introduce the term "minor pieces," used to refer to bishops and knights.

The general rule is that the queen is the strongest piece. She is worth approximately two rooks or three minor pieces. The second most powerful piece is the rook. If you can capture a rook and only give up a bishop or a knight, most of the time you have made a good deal. You could say that you have won the "Exchange."

Bishops and knights have approximately the same value. Both are worth approximately three pawns. In theory, the table here offers a guiding principle. However, it is only for normal cases. If you want to mate the opposing king with a combination, you won't care about winning the Exchange. In addition, bishops and knights can have very different values, depending on how many possible moves the pieces have in a particular situation.

Now you are familiar with the rules of chess and the value of the pieces. The following chapters contain all the important information you'll need to start to understand the complexity and the strategies of chess.

One more word, about the diagrams in this book. We've divided the available space to place the diagrams always at the top of the pages. The text falls on the lower portion of the page. The advantage is that, at the end of each chapter, you can easily examine all the diagrams and the comments in order to review what you have learned. On the other hand, as you read, pay close attention to the diagram numbers in the text so that you look at the correct illustrations!

General Exchange Values		
1 queen	= 9 pawns	= 2 rooks or 3 minor pieces
1 rook	= 5 pawns	= 1 minor piece and 2 pawns
1 bishop	= 3 pawns	= 1 knight
1 knight	= 3 pawns	= 1 bishop

Moves Toward Checkmate

Several of the exercises in the section on the rules showed simple checkmate positions. Of course, mastering the concept of checkmate is very important, but only rarely will you be able to checkmate your opponent in the first few moves. Follow the moves explained here on your own chessboard. Begin with the basic starting position.

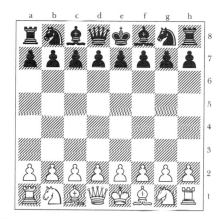

1 White's turn to move: The basic starting position.

Checkmate in the First Few Moves

If you are in a hurry, and you are playing an absolute beginner who never had a chess book, try the following:

1. e2 - e4

This move clears a path for the queen and the bishop. These are the two pieces White wants to use in his surprise attack.

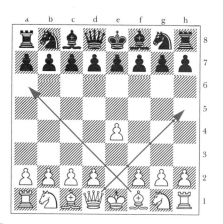

2 After 1. e2 - e4: The path is clear for the queen and the bishop.

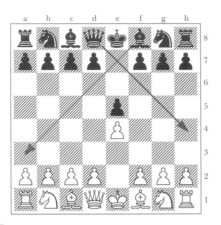

3 After 1. ... e7 - e5: Black will want to move both his queen and bishop.

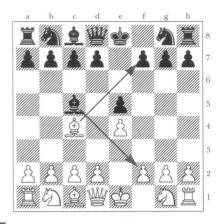

4 After 2. ... Bf8 - c5: White is attacking f7; Black is attacking f2.

1. ...   e7 - e5   **3**

Black frees his queen and bishop. This is a good move for Black, too.

2. Bf1 - c4

As you will see following page 71, in the game 1 example on "Quick Development," it is wise to move your minor pieces, your knights and bishops, forward as soon as possible so that they will dominate more squares. Here, the White bishop is attacking the Black pawn at **f7**. Only the Black king defends the pawn. For the time being, that is sufficient protection because if White's next move is Bc4 x f7+, then Black moves his king from **e8** to **f7** and captures White's bishop for only a pawn.

2. ...   Bf8 - c5   **4**

Black moves his bishop forward also. Thus, he is attacking the White pawn on **f2**, which is just as vulnerable as the Black pawn on **f7**.

3. Qd1 - h5

This isn't exactly a master move. The queen is so valuable that she should retreat from almost every attack by the opponent's pieces in order to protect herself. For that reason, experienced players do not move their queen too early onto squares which could be threatened by the opponent. In this case, though, White has created an enormous threat which Black must defend against.

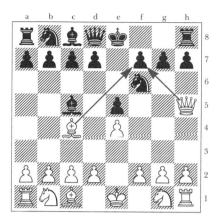

5 After 3. ... Ng8 - f6??: Black forgets about defense.

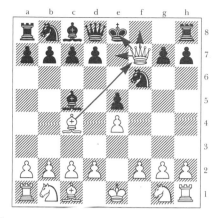

6 After 4. Qh5 x f7: Checkmate after four moves. How embarrassing!

3 ...   Ng8 - f6??   **5**

Black should have protected the square **f7** with Qd8 - e7. Then on the next move, he could have attacked the White queen with Ng8 - f6. This would have warded off the White attack. Now, on the other hand:

4. Qh5 x f7 checkmate   **6**

The king cannot capture the queen since the bishop on **c4** controls square **f7**. The other way to say this is that the bishop is guarding the queen. In addition, the king has no place to go because a move to **f8** or **e7** would put him in check to the White queen. Black has lost because he did not pay attention. This checkmate in four moves is called "Shepherd's Mate," presumably because the person checkmated feels like a dumb sheep.

Here is a second example for a quick checkmate. Similar to the last "game," the loser (Black) is really responsible for his own loss. The example starts from the basic position.

1. e2 - e4   e7 - e5
2. Ng1 - f3

White moves his knight to a square from which he is able to control eight squares. Even though he cannot move to the squares **h2** and **d2** at the moment, he covers the pawns which are standing there. At the same time, he attacks the pawn on **e5**, because *2. Nf3 x e5* is threatened.

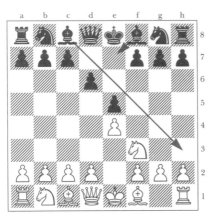

7 After 2. ... d7 - d6: This frees one Black bishop but locks the other one in.

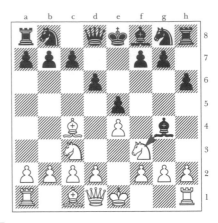

8 After 4. ... Bc8 - g4?: Black overlooks the danger.

2. ...   d7 - d6   **7**

Black defends his pawn on **e5** from 3. Nf3 x e5 because that would make 3. ... d6 x e5 possible. This move, however, does not achieve much otherwise. Even though the bishop now has a clear path on the c8 - h3 diagonal, the pawn on **d6** blocks most of the possible moves for the other Black bishop on **f8**.

3. Bf1 - c4   h7 - h6?

This is a typical beginner's move! Black is afraid that, at some point, one of White's knights or bishops will appear on **g5**. Therefore, as a precaution, he secures the square **g5** with the pawn at **h6**. But in so doing he loses time, which he should have used to activate his pieces; although 3. ... Ng8 - f6? to 4.Nf3 - g5! would have caused problems, because the knight and the bishop would both be threatening square **f7** and the square could

not be defended sufficiently. Black would have done better by moving 3. Bf8 - e7, in order to continue with 4. ... Ng8 - f6 and 5. ... 0 - 0.

4. Nb1 - c3   **8**

White now moves his second knight to a square from which he has many possible moves.

4. ...   Bc8 - g4?

Black moves his bishop to **g4**. He is ready at any time to exchange his bishop for the White knight on **f3** with Bg4 x f3, if this should seem desirable. But Bg4 x f3 is not a real threat because the queen on **d1** and the pawn on **g2** are guarding the knight.

More important, Black has overlooked a decisive possibility for White. White now has three pieces "outside," counting knights, bishops, rooks, and the queen; not the king or the pawns. Black, on the other hand, only has one piece on the outside after Bc8 - g4. So far, Black has made more moves with his pawns than with his pieces. This leads to a quick mating attack.

5. Nf3 x e5!

The surprise! Even though the pawn on **d6** covers the pawn on **e5**, the knight captures. Even more puzzling, the bishop on **g4** could now capture the queen on **d1**. Under normal circumstances, this would produce an advantage that could decide the game. After all, a queen is much more valuable than a bishop. Nevertheless, here it is White who emerges victorious in all of these variations. The move 5. Nf3 x e5 is called a sacrifice.

5. ...   Bg4 x d1??

Would you have captured the queen? Black could not resist the temptation, but he would have done better to capture the knight on **e5**. 5. ... d6 x e5. White would have responded with 6. Qd1 x g4. Black would then have lost one pawn without compensation; and, thus, would be in a losing position. (A losing position is one in which one side will lose in a game played correctly by both sides.) But Black could have continued to fight; and, if his opponent was careless, he could still have won. Now, on the other hand, he will lose very quickly.

6. Bc4 x f7+ Ke8 - e7

The knight on **e5** is covering the bishop on **f7**. Therefore, the king can-

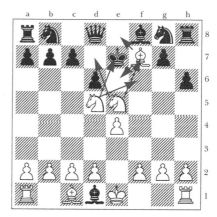

9 After 7. Nc3 - d5 checkmate: White controls all the squares. Checkmate.

not capture the bishop. The Black move is the only one possible.

7. Nc3 - d5 checkmate   **9**

The White pieces work well together in this checkmate. The bishop on **f7** controls squares **e6** and **e8**. The knight on **e5** guards the bishop on **f7** and controls **d7**. The knight on **d5** controls **f6** and checks the king. Black has no legal move, and he is checkmated.

Checkmate in the Endgame

Often, neither player succeeds in defeating the king in a direct attack. Instead, one conquers the other's king because of a material advantage, perhaps only having conquered one pawn more than his opponent. This material superiority will be used to win, often very late in the game, using an elementary move leading to checkmate.

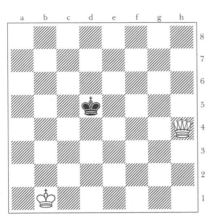

10 White's turn: The Black king is still standing in the center of the board.

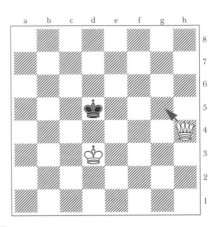

11 After 2. ... Ke5 - d5: Now the queen and king can work together.

Queen and King Against King

In general, you can checkmate a "naked" king with another king and a queen. You need to involve your own king in the battle because, although the queen is the most powerful piece in chess, she cannot succeed in check-mating the king all by herself. **10**

See the diagram above as a starting position, and follow the checkmating through these three phases.

Phase 1: The White king approaches his Black colleague in order to support the White queen in the check-mating process.

1. Kb1 - c2   Kd5 - e5
2. Kc2 - d3   Ke5 - d5   **11**
The Black king wants to stay board center to avoid being checkmated.

Phase 2: The White king and queen push the Black king onto the edge of the board. The queen closes off the center of the board.

3. Qh4 - g5+ Kd5 - e6
4. Kd3 - e4
The White king moves so that he is directly opposite the Black king. This restricts the Black king's field of movement in the center of the board.

4. ...   Ke6 - d6
5. Qg5 - d5+ Kd6 - c7
Covered by her king, the White queen has driven the Black king onto the seventh rank. Now, White must prevent his return to the sixth rank. Therefore:

6. Qd5 - e6   Kc7 - b7
7. Ke4 - d5
The White king rushes to the scene, helping to push the Black king to the edge.

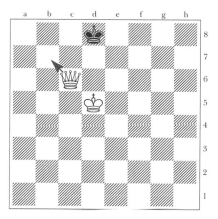

12 After 8. ... Kc7-d8: Pushed to the edge with combined forces.

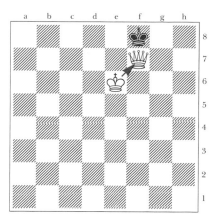

13 After 11. Qb7 - f7 checkmate: The White king guards the queen.

7. ...   Kb7 - c7
8. Qe6 - c6+   Kc7 - d8   **12**
It is done! The Black king stands at the edge of the board.

Phase 3: White attempts to detain the hostile king at the edge of the board and checkmate him.

9. Qc6 - b7
Not 9. **Kd5 - e6??** Stalemate and, therefore, the game would be a draw.

9. ...   Kd8 - e8
10. Kd5 - e6   Ke8 - f8
11. Qb7 - f7 checkmate   **13**

Work with a partner or use your computer chess game to practice checkmating with a king using only your queen and king. This exercise will give you a good feel for how to coordinate the movement of two pieces to checkmate the opponent.

Checkmating with only a king and a rook is somewhat more difficult, as the following example shows.

Rook and King Against King

Just as in checkmating with king and queen, here you also use three phases.

1. Bring your own king close.
2. Push hostile king toward the edge.
3. Keep hostile king at the edge and checkmate.

In this case, the task is more difficult because the rook controls fewer squares than the queen. White, therefore, must move much more precisely. In order to achieve checkmate, he must not only push the Black king to the edge, but also into one of the four corners of the chess board. Diagram 14 shows the starting position.

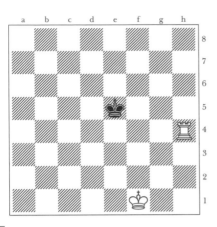

14 White's turn to move: The king on f1 is still too far away from the opponent.

15 After 3. ... Ke5 - f5: With 4. Rd4 - e4, White can now win terrain.

Phase 1:
Bring your king close.   **14**

1. Kf1 - e2   Ke5 - d5
2. Ke2 - d3   Kd5 - e5

Phase 2:
Push the hostile king onto the edge.

3. Rh4 - d4
An important move that denies Black the center of the board.

3. ...   Ke5 - f5   **15**

4. Rd4 - e4
White pursues and immediately cuts off another file from the Black king.

4. ...   Kf5 - f6
Now White has to bring his king into position in order to be able to cut off more squares with his rook.

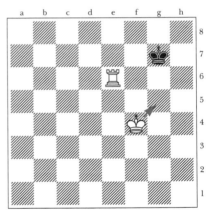

16 After 8. ... Kg6 - g7: The Black king is already on the next to last rank.

5. Kd3 - e3   Kf6 - f5
6. Ke3 - f3   Kf5 - f6

If 7. ...Kf5 - g5, then White would have proceeded with 8. Re4 - e5+.

7. Kf3 - f4   Kf6 - g6
8. Re4 - e6+   Kg6 - g7   **16**

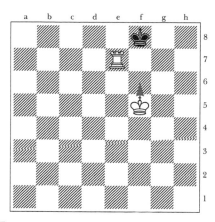

17 After 11. ... Kg7 - f8: Success! The king is on the edge.

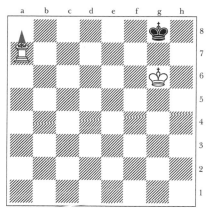

18 After 14. ... Kh8 - g8: White will checkmate Black on the next move.

Of course, 9. Kf4 - f5 also leads to checkmate, but after 9. ... Kg7 - f7, White would first have to make a stalling move (for example 10. Re6 - e1) in order to proceed.

9. ...   Kg7 - f7
10. Kg5 - f5   Kf7 - g7
11. Re6 - e7+   Kg7 - f8   **17**

How would it have continued after 11. ... Kg7 - h6? Do you see the checkmate in two moves? White would have made an observant move to the seventh rank, e.g. 12.Re7 - d7. Black then would have had no choice but to accept 12. ...Kh6 - h5 and the checkmate from 13. Rd7 - h7. In the position after 12. Re7 - d7, Black is in "*zugzwang*," *compelled* to move. This German term is used when every possible move only worsens a player's position. If it were permitted, the player would prefer not to move at all!

Phase 3: Keep the hostile king on the edge, and checkmate.

12. Kf5 - f6   Kf8 - g8
13. Rc7 - a7

The rook remains on the seventh rank to keep the Black king on the edge. Now, in case of 13. ... Kg8 - f8, then 14. Ra7 - a8 checkmate.

13. ...   Kg8 - h8
14. Kf6-g6

This is typical of the movement toward checkmate with a rook and king against a king. White must drive the Black king into the corner where the White king intercepts him. Black has only one legal move. Since chess has no "i" file, the Black king has nowhere to go to escape from the White king.

14. ...   Kh8 - g8   **18**

15. Ra7 - a8 checkmate

You can also checkmate a king with a king and two bishops or with a king, a bishop, and a knight. But these moves toward checkmate would be beyond the scope of a beginner's book. Instead, we would prefer to show how a king and a pawn can be enough to checkmate a king, when the pawn can move to his final square. Have a look at the following example.

Pawn and King Against King

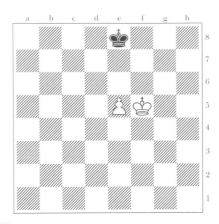

19 Can the pawn be promoted?

Of course, a pawn and king cannot directly produce checkmate. Therefore, the question is always whether or not the pawn can force his way onto his final square. This depends on the exact position and also whose move it is.

Please look at diagram 19: White has advanced with his pawn up to the fifth rank with his king supporting him. Black's king is on the pawn's final square. **19**

In this case, White can only win when it is his move. If it were Black's move, the game would continue like this:

1. ... Ke8 - e7

As you will see later in this game, Black must prevent White's king from continuing to move forward.

2. e5 - e6

White could wait a little while with this move, but without it, he cannot occupy the sixth rank with his king

and he could not improve his position.

2. ... Ke7 - e8!

Only this move will lead to a draw. Black must always move his king to **f8** when the White king is on **f6**. Should Black play 2. ... Ke7 - f8, then 3. Kf5 - f6 Kf8 - e8 4. e6 - e7 Ke8 - d7 5. Kf7 - f7, and on the next turn, White moves 6. e7 - e8 = queen. White's pawn has achieved the promotion. Perhaps it isn't obvious why Black plays 2. ... Ke7 - e8!, but keep following the game.

3. Kf5 - f6 Ke8 - f8

Again, White must try to move his pawn forward.

4. e6 - e7+ Kf8 - e8

What now? The pawn cannot move, and the White king must guard the pawn so that the Black king does not capture him.

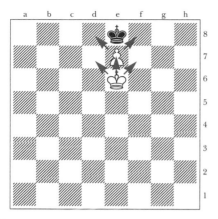

20 After 5. Kf6 - e6 stalemate: Black has no move. Stalemate.

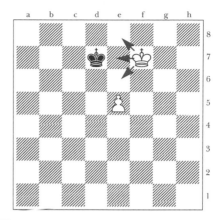

21 After 2. ... Kd8 - d7: King at f7 is in ideal position to control e6, e7, and e8.

5. Kf6 - e6 stalemate **20**

The game is a draw since Black is not in check but has no legal move. He is stalemated. Back to diagram 19. Let's assume that it is White's turn to move. He will win, as follows:

1. Kf5 - e6

The wisest course is to move the king in front of the pawn. Now Black will have to escape to one of the two sides. In other words, Black cannot maintain the face-to-face position of the kings, and the White king can continue to advance.

1. ...   Ke8 - d8
2. Ke6 - f7   Kd8 - d7   **21**

3. e5 - e6+

Now the pawn moves forward! The White king guards the pawn on squares **e6**, **e7**, and **e8**, so that Black

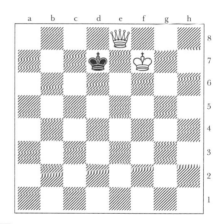

22 After 5. e7 - e8 = queen+: Promotion accomplished!

can no longer prevent the exchange.

3. ...   Kd7 - d8
4. e6 - e7+   Kd8 - d7
5. e7 - e8 = queen+   **22**

White has a new queen. He will soon checkmate Black.

Checkmate in the Middlegame

The most frequent checkmate possibilities occur in the middlegame, and these are the most interesting and most complicated entanglements. We'll show some examples of checkmates that occur quite frequently.

The Back-Rank Checkmate

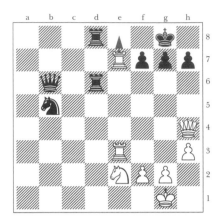

23 White's turn: This shows the back-rank checkmate.

This position has the following characteristics:

❖ Both White rooks control the e-file and so may move one after another to the home rank of the opponent.
❖ Black has only one defender for **e8**, the penetration square.
❖ Black's pawns (**f7**, **g7**, and **h7**) prevent his king from leaving the eighth rank.
❖ Black cannot block the attack after a check by the rook.

White accomplishes the back-rank checkmate in a simple way:

1. Re7 - e8+   Rd8 x e8

2. Re3 x e8 checkmate

By the way, if it had been Black's turn to move in diagram 23, he would not have been able to checkmate White. White has moved his h-pawn to the square **h3**; after 1. ... Rd6 - d1+; therefore, 2.Kg1 - h2 would follow. In situations in which many pieces have been exchanged (i.e., mutually captured), but in which rooks remain on the board, you will want to create some "breathing room" for the king, as White has done with square **h2**.

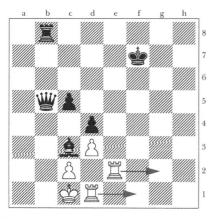

24 White's turn: The rook trap is ready.

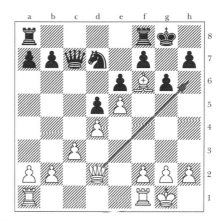

25 White's turn: Black is vulnerable on the squares f6 and h6.

The Two-Rook Checkmate   **24**

Black has a clear material superiority. If it were now his move, the game would finish with <u>1. ...Qb5 - b1 checkmate</u> or <u>1. ...Qb5 - b2 checkmate</u>. However, it is White's turn to move, and his two rooks can checkmate with a popular strategy:

1. Rd1 - f1 +   Kf7 - g6
The king must move to the g-file. Which square he chooses is of no importance; White always wins in the same way.

2. Re2 - g2+   Kg6 - h5
Again it does not matter which square Black chooses on his h-file.

3. Rf1 - h1 checkmate
In this example, the squares on the right side were empty. Black had no chance to escape the rooks. On the

one hand, he could not move any pieces between himself and his attackers; and on the other hand, he could not hide his king behind another man.

Invading Weak Squares   **25**
Here, both players have castled on the short side. Black has moved his pawn onto **g6**. But in doing so, he has weakened the squares **f6** and **h6** because the pawn on **g7** was defending those squares. Now they are unprotected. White has already taken advantage of that by moving his bishop to **f6**, where he takes control of the squares **g7** and **h8**, denying them to the king. However, for a checkmate, White needs another piece.

1. Qd2 - h6
This would not have been possible with a Black pawn on **g7**! White now threatens to checkmate on the next

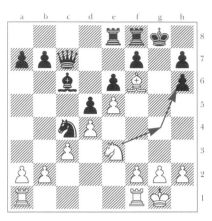

26 White's turn to move: The Black pawn position is a problem.

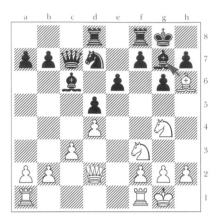

27 White's turn to move: An attack on the Black squares close to the king.

move with 2. Qh6 - g7. Black has only one chance to prevent this.

1. ...   Nd7 x f6
2. e5 x f6
Again, White is threatening to checkmate with *3. Qh6 - g7*, and this time Black can do nothing about it. Black might as well give up.

In general, after you castle, you should not move the pawns directly in front of the king without good reason, because they offer protection. Sometimes you will want to have some *"luft,"* or breathing room (see diagram 23 of this chapter), but each time you move a pawn, you are inviting an opponent to move dangerous attacking pieces into the vacated spot. Remember, once moved, your pawns can never go back!

Here are two more examples on this subject. Diagram 26 shows an unusual situation. Even though Black

still has his queen and White does not, Black cannot prevent checkmate. **26**

1. Ne3 - g4
No matter what Black's move is, 2. Ng4 x h6 checkmate will follow. The missing pawn on **g7**, which clearly captured a piece on **h6**, and the sandwiched position of the Black king make checkmate possible.

In diagram 27, White must remove an obstacle before he can take advantage of weaknesses at the squares **f6**, **g7**, and **h6**. The Black bishop on **g7** defends the weak squares. Therefore, supported by his queen on **d2**, White has moved his bishop to **h6**, in order to exchange pieces with the defender. **27**

1. Bh6 x g7   Kg8 x g7
Now, the queen can join in for the attack.

2. Qd2 - h6+   Kg7 - g8

3. Ng4 - f6+ ?? would be a bad mistake because the knight is unguarded and would simply be lost after 3. ... Nd7 x f6. But White has another possibility:

3. Nf3 - g5

Now, White is threatening checkmate with *4. Qh6 x h7.* The defense 3. ... Nd7 - f6 fails because of 4. Ng4 x f6+.

3. ...   Rf8 - e8

In order to permit the king to escape to **f8**.

4. Qh6 x h7+   Kg8 - f8
5. Qh7 x f7 checkmate

White was able here to attack with a superior force (queen, bishop, and two knights against bishop and knight). A material superiority is often the key to success during an attack on the king.

The Diagonal Attack 28

In this position, White has sacrificed the Exchange, trading one of his rooks for an opposing minor piece. Materially, therefore, Black has an advantage. However, the bishop on **c2** already has a direct line to **h7**. The square **g6** lost its protection when the Black f-pawn was involved in an exchange earlier in the game, and the h-pawn has advanced to **h6**. Therefore, White has the distinct possibility of checkmating on the b1 - h1 diagonal.

1. Qg4 - g6   Nc5 - e4

28 White's turn: The b1 - h7 diagonal is the key to White's victory.

In order to prevent the threatened checkmate with *2. Qg6 - h7,* the knight enters the breach. 1. ... Kh8 - g8 is hopeless since after 2. Rd1 - f1! checkmate is threatened with 3. Qg6 - h7.

2. Nd2 x e4   d5 x e4

Other moves are just as hopeless for Black since White then would keep material superiority and by moving the knight on **e4** onto any square, he would renew the threat of checkmate on **h7**.

3. Bc2 x e4   Kh8 - g8

This is the only way Black can prevent the threat of checkmate on **h7**.

4. Rd1 - f1!

This prevents the retreat of the Black king via the f-file. Now, White is threatening the king again with checkmate on **h7**, and Black can do

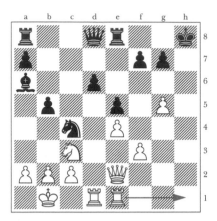

29 White's turn: The open h-file is an invitation to major White pieces.

nothing about it. The queen and bishop have formed a diagonal attack group. Such attacks, especially against square **h7** (or **h2**) are very frequent in chess; therefore, always keep your eye on the b1 - h7 (and b8 - h2) diagonal!

Checkmate Along the Edge   **29**

In diagram 29, no pawns are on the h-file. In other words, the h-file is open. Open lines are "open" invitations to the queen and rooks because they can freely operate there. (We call the queen and the rooks major pieces, as opposed to the bishops and knights, which we call minor pieces.)

In this illustration, White is down a piece, but his major pieces can stage a checkmate attack on the open h-file.

1. Re1 - h1+
White can also play 1. Qe2 - h2+ and then 2. Re1 - h1 in the next move.

1. ...   Kh8 - g8
2. Qe2 - h2
Here, the queen and rook form an attack group. Supported by the rook on **h1**, White now threatens to invade on **h8** along the open h-file and checkmate Black.

2. ...   f7 - f6
This move provides some breathing room for the Black king on **f7**. 2. ... f7 - f5 would receive the same response as the following, and 2. ... Kg8 - f8 3. Nc3 - d5! simply transposes the movement.

3. g5 - g6!
This is better than 3.Qh2 - h8+ Kg8 - f7. With this move, White renews the threat *4. Qh2 - h8 checkmate*.

4. ...   Kg8 - f8
This is the only possibility. Black hopes to be able to flee via **e7**.

5. Nc3 - d5!
The race goes to the swiftest! The knight prevents the flight of the king via **e7**. Now the threat 6. Qh2 - h8 *checkmate* can no longer be warded off.

Attacking, Defending, and Removing Defensive Pieces

The Basic Ideas of Chess Battles

You've seen some examples of how pieces work together in order to checkmate the hostile king. Besides attacking the king, though, there are many other ways to achieve a decisive advantage. Before we move on to page 48 and combinations, we need to examine the following three examples because they show how the attack and defense of pawns and other pieces work in chess.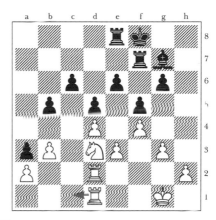

In diagram 1, the Black pawn on **c6** has neither been attacked nor defended. Can White capture it?

1. Rd1 - c1   Rf7 - c7
An attacker (on **c1**) is offset by a defender (on **c7**). Thus, the pawn on **c6** is sufficiently protected.

2. Rd2 - c2
White has staged another attack on the **c7** pawn and now threatens *3. Rc2 x c6 Rc7 x c6. 4. Rc1 x c6.* In case 2. ... c6 - c5 follows, then the pawn is captured after 3. Rc2 x c5.

1 White's turn to move: All men to c6!

2. ...   Re8 - c8
Two attackers (the rooks on **c1** and **c2**) against two defenders (the rooks on **c7** and **c8**). The c- pawn is sufficiently protected again.

3. Nd3 - b4
Now White adds a third attacker, and this time Black has no other defender available. In the next move, White will win the pawn: 3. ... Kg8 - f8   4. Rc2 x c6. Rc7 x c6   5. Rc1 x Rc8 x c6 6. Nb4 x c6. If Black plays

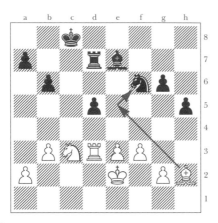

2 White's turn: 1. Bh2 - e5! prepares White to exchange the piece.

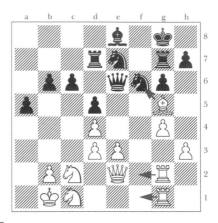

3 White's turn: A material loss despite a sufficient number of defenders.

3. ... c6 - c5, then 4. Rc2 x c5 Rc7 x c5 5. Rc1_x c5 Rc8 x c5 6. d4 x c5. By the way, 3. Nd3 - e5 would have been worse than 3. Nd3 - b4 because then, with 3. ... Bg7 x e5, Black would have gotten rid of the attacker.

In order to see whether a position is sufficiently defended, you must be sure that you have a defender for each attacker. If there are more attackers than defenders, you will lose the man that is under attack.

Of course, your own attacking forces are reduced when you exchange a man for a defender.

Two attackers press the pawn on **d5**, but the rook and the knight are defending him. White captures the pawn by exchanging a defender. **2**

1. Bh2 - e5!

Black now is powerless against the threat *2. Be5 x f6* followed by *3. Nc3 x d5*. But even when their defenders are standing by, merely counting the attackers and defenders is not always enough. (See diagram 3.)

Materially, the two positions are balanced, but Black has a problem here. The knight on **f6** doesn't have a single square he can move to without being captured. He is already threatened by the bishop on **g5**. However, the queen at **e6** still offers him protection, and, if need be, the rooks could also be used for protection. But this security is deceptive. **3**

1. Rg2 - f2   Rg7 - f7

You already see that the sequence of the pieces is not the same. After 1. ... Rd7 - d6, then 2. Rf2 x f6 follows. Even though with 2. ... Qe6 x f6 3. Bg5 x f6 Rd6 x f6 Black could capture, he would lose his queen for a rook in the Exchange! Therefore, the move 1. ... Rg7 - f7 is the only defense.

2. Rg1 - f1

What now? After 2. ... Kg8 - g7 comes 3.Bg5 x f6+ Rf7 x f6 4. Rf2 x f6 Qe6 x f6 5. Rf1 x f6, and Black again would have lost his queen for a rook. Since the knight still does not have a safe square to flee to, the only solution would be:

2. ...   Rd7 - d6

But now White can play:

3. Rf2 x f6   Rf7 x f6
4. Rf1 x f6   Qe6 x f6

Black would be better off moving his queen away, even though White would then have one more piece.

5. Bg5 x f6   Rd6 x f6

After the smoke clears, White has won a queen for a rook. Black simply was not able to counterattack in the right sequence. If he were positioned so that his queen could capture last, then the defense would still have been intact. Therefore, when you are considering the defense of your pieces, be careful that your opponent does not gain materially during an exchange. Otherwise, a piece that you think is guarded isn't really protected at all.

In many situations, the simple attacks discussed in this chapter do not lead to success. Chess is suspenseful because of the many tricks you can use to surprise your opponent.

Combination Moves — A Chess Player's Big Bag of Tricks

The Double Attack

The White knight on **d5** is right in the middle of the board, and he has many possible moves.

In diagram 4, with...

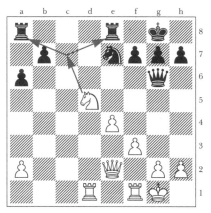

1. Nd5 - c7??
...White can start a double attack against both rooks. White makes a knight fork, one of the most frequent tactical plays. Black will not be able to rescue both rooks; so White will win the Exchange, or so it seems. But not every double attack is advantageous:

1. ...   Qg6 - b6+!
For his part, Black starts his own double attack. He attacks White's king and knight at the same time with his queen. The first thing White has to do is escape from check. No matter how he does this, he loses his knight on **c7** and also his hoped-for gain of the exchange.

2. Qe2 - f2   Qb6 x c7
Black has one more knight and should easily win this game.

The pawn fork is another double attack, and it is as well known as the knight fork. You'll find an example in diagram 5, where the situation is complicated.

White is one pawn down. In addi-

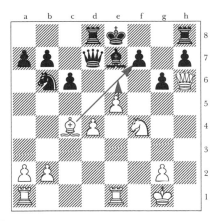

5 White's turn to move: The pawn fork: 1. Bc4 x f7+! besides 2. e5 - e6+.

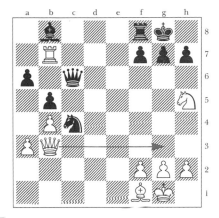

6 White's turn to move: White wins. You need to think about the entire board!

tion, *1. ... Nb6 x c4* and *1. ...Qd7 x d4+* threaten. But the White pieces are standing by, and Black has not yet castled. As a result, Black's king comes under attack in the center of the board.

1. Bc4 x f7+! **5**
White sacrifices his bishop in order to force the Black king into the pawn fork.

1. ...   Ke8 x f7
2. e5 - e6+ **5**
The pawn attacks the queen and king at the same time. Black has to get out of check, and, therefore, loses his queen.

In the following example, you need a wider look at the board. The Black queen is threatening the White rook on **b7**. However, the enormous force of the queen makes a comprehensive double attack possible for White. **6**

1. Rb7 x b8!   Rf8 x b8
White has sacrificed the exchange, but he wins with a double attack.

2. Qb3 - g3
This poses two decisive threats: *3. Qg3 x g7 checkmate* and *3. Qg3 x b8+*. Black has no way to ward off both threats.

You see, when you use a double attack, in many cases your opponent can ward off only one of the threats, and you can then execute the other.

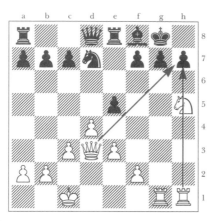

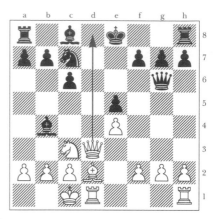

7 White's turn: 1. Qd3 x h7+! leads to dis-covered then double check. Checkmate!

8 White's turn: Queen and rook are on d-file, but bishop on d2 is in the way.

Now, we'll discuss two tactics which are not used as frequently as the double attack, but which can be just as effective. In many cases, they are connected to a double attack.

The Discovered Check and the Double Check

You can see a discovered check in the example. **7**

In diagram 7, White has sacrificed a piece in order to assume a promising attack position. All the White pieces point toward the Black king. Pay attention to the rook on **h1** and the knight on **h5**. If the Black king were standing on **h7**, any move of the **h5** knight would mean that the rook on **h1** would check the king. With ...

1. Qd3 x h7+!

... he sacrifices the queen in order to lure the hostile king into a dis-covered check. This forces the situation.

1. ...   Kg8 x h7

Now the knight on **h5** can make any move he likes. Black will always be in check because of the rook on **h1**. White chooses the best discovered check:

2. Nh5 - f6++ checkmate

This discovered check is also a double check because the rook on **h1** and the knight on **f6** are checking at the same time. In order to ward off a double check, you always must move the king. But here, no legal move is possible for the king—checkmate.

In diagram 8, Black has not yet castled, and White's queen and rook are on the open d-file, ready to attack. Unfortunately, Black's bishop on **d2** stands between them; otherwise, 1. Qd3 - d8 checkmate could follow. But White has no time to withdraw the bishop because that would give Black time to protect his king (e.g. with 1. ... 0 - 0). Therefore, fast action is necessary. White wins with a double check. First, White forces the Black king to **d8**.

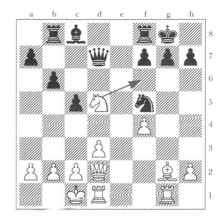

9 **White's turn to move: The rook on g1 toys with the king on g8.**

1. Qd3 - d8+!! Ke8 x d8
White forced the Black move. The sole purpose of the sacrifice of the White queen was to lure the Black king to **d8**. Now for the double check.

2. Bd2 - g5++
The rook on **d1** and the bishop on **g5** check the king! Now Black cannot capture the bishop with his queen, because if he does that, the king will still be in check from the rook on **d1**. Only moving the king will help.

2. ... Kd8 - e8
3. Rd1 - d8 checkmate
The double check often makes it possible for the attacker to move pieces onto squares that seem to be well guarded. Therefore, alarm bells should go off immediately when a double check becomes possible in a game.

The following example shows that a simple discovered check can be enormously effective. The players have the same material, but because of his well-positioned knight on **d5** and his rook on **g1**, White has an

opportunity to stage an attack on the Black king. His goal is an effective discovered check.

1. Nd5 - f6+ ! g7 x f6
The White check was also a knight fork. If 1. ... Kg8 - h8, then the White knight captures the queen on **d7**.

2. Bg2 - c6+
This is a discovered check because even though White has moved the bishop from **g2**, he checks with another piece, the rook on **g1**.

2. ... Kg8 - h8
Black must get out of check, but now the queen falls victim to the bishop.

3. Bc6 x d7
White has a decisive material advantage thanks to the discovered check, 2. Bg2 - c6+.

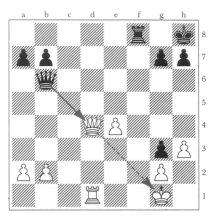

10 Black's turn to move: The White queen on d4 is pinned.

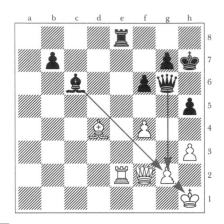

11 Black's turn to move: The c6 - h1 diagonal smells like a combination!

The Pin

When a piece cannot move because it is shielding a more valuable piece, we say that the piece is pinned. Diagram 10 shows an example of how one piece can pin another.

The White queen on **d4** cannot move from the diagonal b6 - g1 or the Black queen will check. So we say that the White queen is pinned. This makes the following winning move possible: **10**

1. ... Rf8 - d8!
2. Qd4 x d8+ fails because the rules state that you cannot make any move that would leave you in check. In order to save his queen, White has only one move:

2. Qd4 x b6 Rd8 x d1 checkmate
When your opponent captures, you don't have to hit back immediately on the same square. For example, 2. ... a7 x b6?? would be a catastrophic mistake because after 3. Rd1 x d8 checkmate, the game result would be overturned. The move, 2. ... Rd8 x d1 checkmate, is called *zwischenzug*, a German term meaning "intermediate move." The normal reaction would be to take the queen. Instead, Black has checkmated by winning the rook.

The position above stems from a game played by Kotov and Botvinnik in 1939. The future world champion, Botvinnik, saw that he could use the c6 - h1 diagonal for a winning pin. **11**

1. ...   Qg6 x g2+!
2. Qf2 x g2
If Botvinnik had simply continued with 2. ... Bc6 x g2+, then White would have moved 3. Re2 x g2, and Black would have suffered material losses. However, there is a stronger play:

2. ...   Re8 x e2
The bishop on **c6** is now pinning the queen on **g2**. She cannot countercapture on **e2**, because then the White king would be in check. White gives up at this point. Even though he has a clear material advantage, he cannot save his queen because of the pin. After 3. Qg2 x c6 b7 x c6, he would be in a hopeless situation, with fewer major pieces and two pawns down.

Diagram 12 shows a position from a game between Alekhine and Nimzowitsch played in San Remo in 1930. The knight on **c6** is in a critical position. If Black were to move this piece, e.g., with 1. ... Nc6 x b4??, then White would have a choice whether to take the material advantage with 2. Rc3 x c7 or with 2. Bb5 x d7+. The knight is actually pinned in several ways and may not move. On the other hand, four White pieces (bishop, queen, and both rooks) are attacking the knight on **c6**. Meanwhile, the other Black knight, the queen, and both rooks are defending the knight. Here are Alekhine's moves: 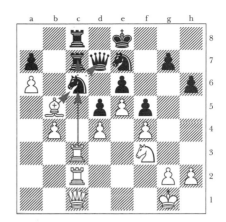 12

12 White's turn to move: The knight at **c6** is pinned by several White pieces.

1. Bb5 - a4!
After Black plays a waiting game with 1. ...g7 - g6, White would play 2. b4 - b5. Black could not save the knight at **c6** from the attack of the pawn since he is still pinned on the c-file. After 2. ... Nc6 - b8, White would react with three attackers (both rooks and the queen) against the rook at **c7**, which is only defended by the Black rook and the queen. White, therefore, would win a rook with 3. Rc3 x c7 Rc8 x c7 4. Rc2 x c7.

1. ...   Ke8 - d8
This is the only defense. Black has to make this move so he can move the knight at **c6** away in case of b4 - b5. To do so, he must be sure the rook on **c7** will be sufficiently defended.

Now, in case of 2. b4 - b5 Nc6 - b8 3.Rc3 x c7 Rc8 x c7 4.Rc2 x c7 Qd7 x c7   5. Qc1 x c7 Kd8 x c7, Black does not lose any material.

2. h2 - h4!

White wins the game in an elegant way. He still has the knight on **c6** pinned. If the knight moves, then the bishop on **b5** would capture the Black queen. The knight at **e7**, the two Black rooks, and the Black queen cannot move either, because if they do, the knight at **c6** would no longer be sufficiently defended and would simply be captured by 3. *Ba4 x c6*. In addition, the king on **d8** cannot move because that would result in a new pin in the c-file. Therefore, after 2. ... Kd8 - e8, 3. b4 - b5 would capture the knight. Thus, one of the Black pieces must move or Black will suffer a material loss. Since all of the pawn moves are quickly exhausted, Black is forced to move a piece. Any move he makes will only worsen his position, so he is in "zugswang."

2. ...   h6 - h5
3. Kg1 - h2   g7 - g6
4. g2 - g3   resigns   **13**

Have a closer look at this position. Even though White is not threatening, Black cannot avoid a material loss in each of his next moves. The pin of the knight on **c6** has made this impressive victory possible. Pay attention to the fact that pinned pieces are especially vulnerable to attack because their movement is seriously restricted. They only seem to be guarding other pieces, but in fact they are bound to stay where they are.

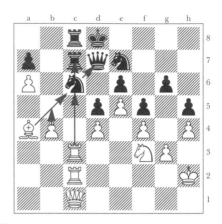

13 Forced to move, Black suffers a material loss.

The Diversion

A position from a game played by Botvinnik and Keres in Moscow in 1966 follows. Notice that White has moved a pawn far forward to **g6**. To safely capture the pawn on **h4** with his queen would be decisive. Then, Black could not prevent checkmate. But unfortunately, the Black queen on **d8** is guarding the pawn on **h4**. Can White somehow divert her?   **14**

1. Rb1 - b8!

This is a typical diversion sacrifice. The White move has only one purpose: to entice the queen to give up the position which guards the Black pawn on **h4**.

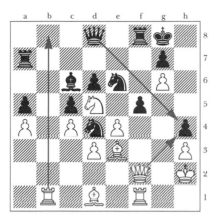

14 White's turn: If Black queen moves from d8, then Qf2 x h4 would be decisive.

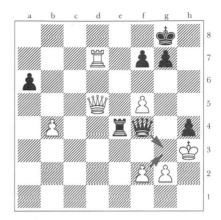

15 Black's turn: "How do I get to 2. ... Qf4 - g3 checkmate?"

1. ...   Qd8 x b8

The rook on **b8** is attacking the queen. The White minor pieces control squares **e7**, **f6**, and **g5**. Therefore, Keres has no way to continue guarding the pawn at **h4**. He captures the rook and has finished himself off.

2. Qf2 x h4

Now, White threatens checkmate with 3. *Qh4 - h7*. Here, Keres resigned. The game could have continued:

2. ...   Rf8 - e8

2. ... Ne6 - g5   3. Be3 x g5 or 2. ... Qb8 - b2+   3.Kh2 - h1 does not change the situation. With 2. ... Rf8 - e8, Black gives his king some breathing room.

3. Qh4 - h7+   Kg8 - f8
4. Qh7 - h8 checkmate

Here is another example of how a diversion sacrifice can win the game. This is from a game between Tarjan and Karpov in Skopje, Yugoslavia, in 1976. At that time, Karpov was already the world champion. In general, he only used sacrifices when he was sure to gain an advantage. Here, the situation is clear cut. White threatens to checkmate Black with *Qd5 x f7+* followed by *Qf7 x g7*. Black would like to play 1. ...Qf4 - g3+, but the pawn on **f2** controls **g3**.   **15**

1. ...   Re4 - e3+ !

A diversion sacrifice. White resigned. After 2. f2 x e3, 2. ... Qf4 - g3 checkmate follows. Checkmate also follows 2. f2 - f3. Even 2. Qd5 - f3 Re3 x f3+ is hopeless. The only possibility is:

2. g2 - g3   Re3 x g3+!
3. Kh3 - h2

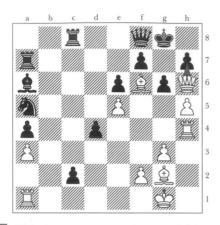

16 White's turn to move: How can White activate the bishop at g2?

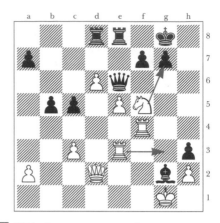

17 White's turn to move: Nf5 x g7! opens the White position.

Or 3. f2 x g3   Qf4 x g3 checkmate.

3. ...   Qf4 x f2 +
4. Kh2 - h1   Qf2 - g2 checkmate

The Demolition Sacrifice

Diagram 16 shows a position from a 1967 game between world champion Fischer and Miagmasuren in Sousse, Tunisia. The accumulation of White pieces near the Black king looks threatening, but Black has just moved his queen to **f8** in order to exchange the most dangerous attacker, the White queen on **h6**. Fischer did not want to have anything to do with the trade. He moved: **16**

1. Qh6 x h7+!   Kg8 x h7
2. h5 x g6++
This creates a discovered double check from the rook and pawn. It also demolishes the Black pawn defense on the king's side. In case of 2. ...Kh7 - g8, then 3. Rh4 - h8 checkmate.

2. ...   Kh7 x g6
3. Bg2 x e4 checkmate
Notice that initially, the bishop on **g2** has no chance to participate in the attack. However, with his demolition sacrifice on **h7** and the subsequent elimination of the pawn on **g6**, Fisher ensured that this bishop would become decisive in his attack.

Finally, here's a relatively complicated example which shows a demolition that does not lead to checkmate quite so quickly. Diagram 17 shows the positions of two future world champions, Spassky and Smyslov, during a 1953 game in Bucharest, Romania. By the way, Spassky was sixteen years old at the time.

Spassky, playing White, is one pawn down. But two factors more than compensate for that. First, his pieces are ready for an attack on the king. Black, on the other hand, has only a few forces to defend the squares around his king.

Second, White has a pawn far forward on **d6**. None of Black's pawns can block or capture this pawn on his way to the eighth rank. Therefore, the other Black pieces must try to delay his progress or eventually the pawn will be promoted to a major piece.

We call a pawn in this position a free pawn or a passed pawn. Because they must constantly prevent the White pawn on **d6** from advancing, the Black pieces are limited in what they can do. Thus, even though Black is one pawn up, White is bound to win. Spassky won using a demolition sacrifice.

1. Nf5 x g7! `17`

This removes the Black g-pawn, allowing Spassky to prepare for his major pieces to take action. Spassky's move is a demolition sacrifice because it demolishes the pawn defense in front of the hostile king, allowing Spassky to start an attack. At the same time, the knight on **g7** forks Smyslov's Black queen and rook.

1. ...   Rd8 x d6

In a losing position, Smyslov tries one more trick: By countersacrificing his rook, he attacks the White queen on **d2**. He must have hoped to confuse his young opponent that way. 1. ...Kg6 x g7 is followed by 2. Re3 - g3+ Kg7 - f8. (If Black plays 2. ... Qe6 - g6 and thus gives up his queen, he will clearly lose.) 3. Rf4 x f7+! Qe6 x f7 (or 3. ... Kf8 x f7 4. Qd2 - f4+ Qe6 - f6 5. Qf4 x f6 checkmate). 4. Qd2 - h6+ Qf7 - g7 5. Qh6 x g7 checkmate.

2. Ng5 x e6!

Spassky, of course, realized that his e-pawn was pinned. Using 2. e5 x d6?? Qe6 x e3+ or 2. Qd2 x d6 Qe6 x d6 3. e5 x d6 Re8 x e3 would have been completely wrong. Smyslov resigned after 2. Ng5 x e6! Had he not, the game would have continued:

2. ...   Rd6 x d2
3. Re3 - g3+

As a result of 1. Nf5 x g7!, the g-file is open for the rook to check.

3. ...   Kg8 - h8
4. Rf4 - h4 checkmate

A demolition sacrifice has to be calculated very carefully if you cannot mate your opponent immediately. However, if you are able to destroy the pawn protection in front of the hostile king, your attacking pieces can be more effective.

Test 2: Combinations

The following combination exercises may give you quite a headache. After all, the victorious parties were world champions.

Below each exercise you'll find the method used by the winning player. Unless you are an unusually talented player, you probably won't be able to solve the exercises without another hint. Don't despair if the right moves don't come easily to you. Simply have a look at Tip 1 under the exercise. Hopefully, it will lead you to the answer. But if it doesn't, try Tip 2.

I recommend that you use a piece of paper to cover up the tips while you look at the exercise. In all the exercises, you can achieve checkmate or a very clear material gain in a few moves.

1 Black's turn to move: Mating attack.

Game: Thorez – Alekhine, Seville, 1922
With a mating attack, Black wins at least one piece.

Tip 1   In the course of the solution, Black uses a double check.

Tip 2   The first move is 1. ... Qh5 x h3.

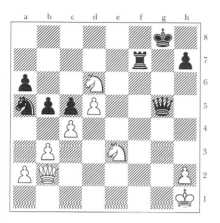

2 White's turn to move: White achieves a decisive material gain.

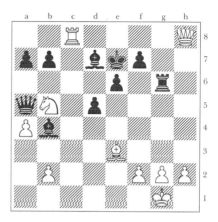

3 White's turn to move: What is the idea of 1. Be3 - b6!!?

Game: Petrosian – Spassky, Moscow, 1966

After 1. Nd6 x f7? Qg5 x e3, White has no direct win. How can White quickly achieve a decisive material superiority?

Tip 1 The method is a knight fork.

Tip 2 White must sacrifice the queen in order to prepare the knight fork.

Game: Tal – name unknown, Soviet Union, 1964

After White's move, 1. Be3 - b6 !!, Black can capture the bishop with the pawn or with the queen. How does White play after 1. ... a7 x b6 ? How does he play after 1. ... Qa5 x b6 ?

Tip 1 After 1. ... a7 x b6 the Black queen does not control **c7** and **d8** anymore. After 1. ... Qa5 x b6, the bishop on **b4** is unguarded.

Tip 2 1. ... a7 x b6 creates checkmate in one move. 1. ... Qa5 x b6 sets up a double attack through the White queen.

| Exercise 4 | Exercise 5 |

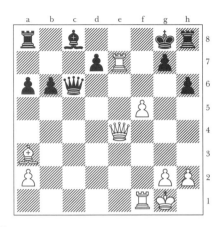

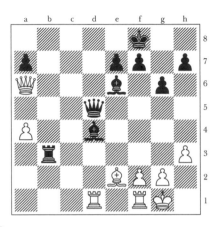

4 White's turn: White checkmates.

5 Black's turn: Checkmate attack.

Game: Morphy – name unknown, New Orleans, 1858

White can start a forceful attack here.

Tip 1 White wins with a demolition sacrifice.

Tip 2 In the end, the queen checkmates the king all by herself since the Black king is hemmed in on the edge by his own pieces.

Game: Bareyev – Kasparov, Paris, 1991

With 1. … Be6 x h3, Black could achieve a strong attack, but he has an even more forceful continuation to force checkmate.

Tip 1 Pinning the pawn at **f2** makes an unusual move possible.

Tip 2 The checkmate takes place on **g2**. After the first Black move, White has no defense anymore because, after that, the pawn on **f2** and the pawn on **g2** are pinned.

If Chess Pieces Could Talk

Sometimes, while watching a chess tournament, you notice a strong master player observing a game between two weak players. After certain moves, he makes a sour face, as if he had been forced to drink lemon juice. You can almost hear him say, "Yuck!" Most of the time, this reaction is caused by the complete misunderstanding of the position by one of the two players involved. In other words, by a move that even the chess pieces themselves would protest against—if they could talk.

But the fact that chess pieces can't talk won't prevent us from hearing them speak here and now. Let's hear what the pawns have to say:

Demands of the Pawns

You beginners don't give us enough attention. You would probably like it if your own pawns would simply disappear so that your pieces would have a clear path. But don't forget that each of us can be promoted to a queen! Therefore, you had better pay attention when one of us is threatened. And something else, too. Some of you seem

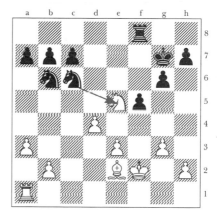

1 Black's turn to move: Who ends up with the doubled pawn?

to believe that it doesn't matter whether we are standing in front of each other or next to each other. Have a look at the diagram. **1**

In this game, I was the pawn on **b7**. I did not have any special worries. Even though White had a powerful knight on **e5**, my player could simply move 1. ... Nc6 x e5, and everything would be fine. After 2. d4 x e5, White would have had two pawns in front of each other on the e-file. We call this situation doubled pawns. The White doubled pawns on **e3** and **e5** would have been isolated; no other pawn

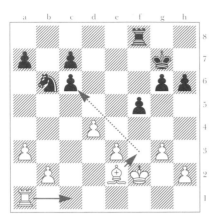

2 White's turn to move: Notice the isolated doubled pawns on c6 and c7.

would have been able to guard either of them. I had already imagined everything:

With 2. ... Rf8 - e8   3. Ra1 - c1 (an attack on my colleague at **c7**), 3. ... c7 - c6   4. Rc1-c5 (in order to defend **e5**), 4. ...Nb6 - d7, we would have simply taken the White pawn on **e5**. I was in good spirits, but do you know what my player did?

1. ...   h7 - h6??

Not only does he not give doubled pawns to White, he also lets me slide into trouble on the c-file. White was smarter. He took a deep breath and mumbled something about being incredibly lucky. Then the game continued like this:

2. Ne5 x c6   b7 x c6

And there I was, on **c6**, in front of my own colleague. Obviously, they all attacked me.

3. Ra1 - c1   Rf8 - f6

Gradually, my player realized what was going on. But by that time, he already looked grumpy. My friend, the pawn on **c7**, really wanted to guard me, but when we are standing in front of each other, there isn't anything we can do for each other.

4. Be2 - f3

Oh no, another one! I was getting sick. I had no other defenders. Therefore, my player now tried:

4. ...   Nb6 - d5

to prevent the bishop on **f3** from capturing **c6**. Even though he saved my life with this move, the remainder of the game was no fun. White answered with:

5. Bf3 x d5   c6 x d5
6. Rc1 x c7+

My friend, the pawn on **c7**, went off to the dark little box, muttering angrily to himself. With one more pawn, White easily won the game.

Please make sure that we pawns do not have such a difficult life. Don't let us become doubled pawns without a good reason. Make sure that, whenever possible, a neighboring pawn can guard us. If you'll do this for us, we'll be happy to fight your battles!

2

Demands of the Bishops

Sometimes, when we bishops have free diagonals, we can be enormously strong, certainly stronger than the

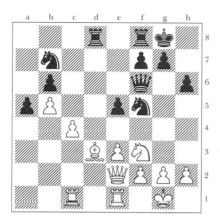

3 White's turn to move: The bishop on d3 is still alive.

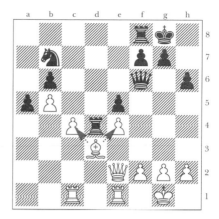

4 After 2. ... Rd8 x d4: The bishop at d3 is essentially downgraded to a pawn.

short-legged knights. They need too much time to jump from one edge of the board to the next. Unfortunately, players frequently really hem us in, and we hardly have room to breathe. Here is an example. **3**

Here, I am the bishop on **d3**. To be honest, my player was not especially satisfied with this position. Even though the two sides are even, Black already has a rook on the open d-file, and the White rooks are still blocked by their own pawns. In addition, the Black a-pawn could advance later in the game. Our pawns can neither block him nor capture him on his way to **a1**, where he wins promotion. Nevertheless, I did not worry too much. If need be, I was ready, after 1. Bd3 x f5, to watch the game from the little box. However, I hoped that my player would play 1. Qe2 - c2. Then, we would have worked the b1 - h7 diagonal. In addition, 1. Bd3 - e4 was

okay with me as a way for me to move to **d5**. However, when I saw that my player was seriously contemplating the e-pawn, I had a bad feeling ...

1. c3 - e4??
As a human being, you cannot imagine what it is like when a huge pawn blocks my view. Until then, I was able to look up to **h7**. After that, I could see nothing but walls. Actually, I felt like a pawn myself because I could only guard **e4** and **c4** in front of me. My player had no understanding of what he had done to me. Oh well, he was soon to realize that he had handed Black all the cards. Purely from annoyance, I fell over, but, of course, that did not help.

1. ...   Nf5 - d4
2. Nf3 x d4   Rd8 x d4   **4**
Do you see White's problems? First of all, I can hardly move anymore, and

63

I cannot move to the squares where I could be of some service. The second problem with the 1. e3 - e4?? move is that White cannot control square **d4** anymore. All my life, I have been a White-square bishop. As hard as I try, I will never be able to defend the Black squares. Thus, when my Black-square colleague was exchanged, our pawns had to pay attention to the important dark squares, for example to **d4**, or the dark squares become defenseless. In the name of all bishops, I make the following demand: When a player has only one bishop left, his central pawns should stand on squares of the opposite color. This will prevent a further invasion and give maximum freedom to the remaining bishop.

Let's watch the end of the game to see how Black exploited the weaknesses of our dark squares, and how useless I was, simply standing around.

3. Re1 - d1   Rf8 - d8
4. Bd3 - c2

My player really wanted to exchange the strong hostile rooks.

4. ...   Qf6 - e6
Here the queen is attacking **c4**.

5. Rd1 x d4   Rd8 x d4
6. Bc2 - b1

I have to find somewhere to get out of the way so that the rook on **c1** can guard the pawn on **c4**. At this point, I can only dream of attacking a hostile pawn. Things are quite different for the Black knight:

6. ...   Nb7 - c5
What a life he has! He is completely safe, and he is attacking the pawn on **e4**. He is also threatening to cause trouble at **d3** or **b3**.

7. h2 - h3
My player has no ideas anymore and is simply killing time. He cannot think of any way to counterattack, and Black dominates the board.

7. ...   Qe6 - d7
8. Bb1 - c2   Rd4 - d2

Black penetrates the second rank and lands, of course, on another Black square.

9. Qe2 - e1   Qd7 - d4
Now the Black queen is boss: She is standing unassailably in the center of the board, guarding **d2** and controlling **a1** and **f2** among others.

10. g2 - g3
White has no more opportunities. He can only wait to see how Black claims the victory.

10. ...   a5 - a4
11. Kg1 - g2   a4 - a3
12. h3 - h4   a3 - a2

Here's where my player resigned. He couldn't stop the a-pawn without destroying his position.

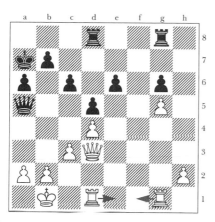

5 White's turn to move: The White rooks are still passive.

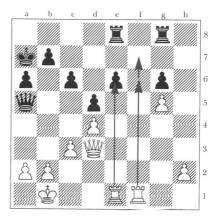

6 After 2. Rg1 - f1: The White rooks are on the move.

Demands of the Rooks

We rooks like to stay in the background. We rarely feel comfortable in the turmoil of the battle. Because we are more valuable than bishops and knights, we have to flee when a minor piece attacks us. Often beginners don't know what to do with us. Yet, with a little bit of effort, we can be very helpful. You only need to place us on an open line.

Look at diagram 5. I was the rook on **g1**. I was not especially pleased with my position because the pawn on **g5** was still blocking me. The rook on **d1** was not any happier, because there were no targets for him to attack on the d-file. Luckily, we had a reasonable player who moved us to much better squares. **5**

1. Rd1 - e1
Instead of passively standing on the d-file, this rook can now threaten the pawn on **e6**. That's the way it works. We rooks must move in a straight line.

1. ... Rd8 - e8
2. Rg1 - f1 **6**
Finally, I can see again! I feel better on **f1** because the line is completely free. This freedom gives me fantastic possibilities. Compare the positions of us White rooks with the Black ones on **g8** and **e8**. They lead a sad life. They are not standing on open lines, and they can only defend their own pawns.We, on the other hand, are active and flexible.

2. ... Qa5 - c7
3. Rf1 - f6
This is fun! With this move, I could pose a double threat: *4. Rf6 x e6* and *4. Rf6 x g6*. In any case, Black will

lose a pawn. Thus, you must remember not to leave us on unproductive squares! If there are no open lines for us, then please try to open the way for us by advancing a pawn.

Demands of the Knights

People often call us horses. Although we take a long time to jump from one end of the board to the other, we are very contented animals because we can simply jump over the other pieces to reach our goal. However, in some games we are hopelessly stranded because the player does not know how to move us to active squares. Note, for instance, the situation in diagram 7.

If you had a choice, which of the four knights would you like to be? Certainly not the knight on **h8**. From his position in the corner, he only has two possible moves. In truth, he cannot move to **g6** because two pawns are threatening that square, and he cannot go to **f7** because it is already occupied by the Black queen. The knight on **a5** seems to be in a slightly better position. From his position on the edge, he dominates four squares, but he is unguarded and has no safe retreat. Now, on to me, the knight on **e3**. I dominate eight squares, which is the maximum. At this time, though, only two of them (**c2** and **d1**) are free. However, from my central position, I will surely have good possibilities during the course of the game. The

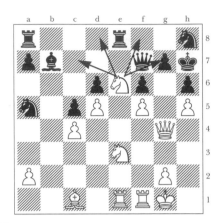

7 White's turn: The e6 knight has all moves; a5 and h8 knights are stranded.

showpiece of the White position is clearly the knight on **e6**. Like me, he also dominates eight squares. In addition, the pawns on **d5** and **f5** guard his position. He is in the middle of the board and far enough in the opponent's camp that he can even participate in an attack on the king by guarding square **g7** with the White queen. Black quickly lost this game because the White knights were far superior to the Black ones. **7**

1. Bc1 - d2

This move attacks the knight **a5**. And the knight can not be defended anymore, since 1. ... Qf7 - c7 fails at 2. Ne6 x c7. Each flight would also lead to the loss of the knight. Therefore, in order to remove the strong knight at **e6,** Black must sacrifice the exchange.

1. ...   Re8 x e6
2. f5 x e6   Qf7 - c7

At least Black was able to save the knight on the edge. However, now the knight on **h8** has no chance at all to come out of the corner since he would be captured on **g6** and on **f7** by a White pawn. Now it's my turn!

3. Ne3 - f5

I take advantage of the fact that the pawn has moved from **f5** to **e6**. On **f5**, I am almost as strong as my brother, the knight on **e6**, was before. I am looking at **d6**, **g7**, and **h6**. That way, I can support the continued advance of the e-pawn as well as the attack on the king. We threaten *4. Bd2 x a5 Qc7 x a5 5.Qg4 x g7 checkmate.*

3. ...   Re8 - g8

This move covers up the weak point at **g7**.

4. e6 - e7

The e-pawn is on his way to promotion! Black is completely pinned. His rook must guard **g7**, his queen must guard the knight at **a5**, both his knights are useless, and the e-pawn,

supported by the rook on **e1**, is threatening to move to **e8** and be promoted to another queen. No matter how Black moves, he will suffer a material loss. His position is really hopeless.

When you are in doubt, move us knights to a square in the center of the board rather than to an edge square. Once we are securely stationed in the hostile half of the board, we are able to decide many games almost all on our own.

Demands of the Queens

We are, by far, the most powerful pieces in chess, and we want to be treated with respect. Kindly refrain from giving us nicknames. Simply refer to us as "the queens" or, if you like, call us "ladies."

A player who enters the turmoil of the battle must seriously consider what he is doing. Of course we are at hand for every job, from capturing pawns to checkmating the opponent's king. But, frequently, instead of being the hunter, we become the hunted. That is really degrading. For instance, have a look at the example on page 68.

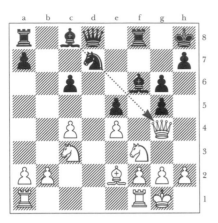

8 White's turn: Notice the knight on **d7** between the **c8** bishop and **g4** queen.

The position in diagram 8 comes from a game which was part of a "Chess Olympics." White has one more pawn, but the bishop on **e2** is imprisoned (see "Demands of the Bishops"), and if the knight on **d7** moves, the bishop on **c8** will threaten me. **8**

Even though Black has doubled pawns in the g-file, he is well defended, and the exposed position of the White queen is the main problem in the position. White should secure me with 1. Qg4 - g3 or place a rook on the open d-file with 1. Rf1 - d1, which would pin the knight on **d7** (with the rook on **d1** facing the queen on **d8**). Instead, White decided to use

1. Qg4 - e6??

to catch a pawn, threatening 2. Qe6 x c6. But we queens are so valuable that we only feel really safe when we

cannot be threatened at all. Here, the situation isn't good.

1. ...   Nd7 - b8!

From **b8**, the knight covers the pawn on **c6**. In addition, the bishop on **c8** attacks me. Despite my many possible moves, I have no square to move to where I would not be captured. White lost me and the game.

As White discovered, such carelessness toward us ladies, in chess as in life, causes problems. If a queen is on the same diagonal as a hostile bishop or on the same line as a hostile rook, your alarm bells should go off. Of course, the same holds true of fork threats from pawns or knights. We can be captured this way. Only those players who are able to protect us, as well as use our power, will be successful in chess!

His Eminence, the King

What we kings must endure! Instead of entering the battle as powerful rulers, we are humiliated and turned into victims who are basically defenseless. For a change, we would like to be able to move as much as the queens, bishops, and rooks do! Then we wouldn't be checkmated so quickly.

But since this is only a dream, you should keep an eye on your king. Be sure his position is secure. When the opponent moves several pieces close to your king, when hostile rooks on open lines can support an attack on

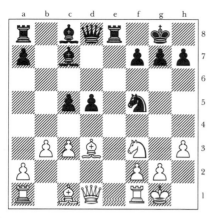

9 White's turn to move: The line of pawns in front of both kings is intact.

the king, or when a bishop and the queen form a diagonal attack group, sound the trumpets! Defenders, rally around your king! Players often, unfortunately, destroy the line of pawns in front of the king for no reason at all. Then they have to chase away hostile pieces.

Diagram 9 shows an especially annoying example.

Actually, White has nothing special to fear. The pieces are balanced, and both sides have free diagonals for their bishops. However, the Black rook on **e8** already has an open line, while both White rooks are still standing rather passively. In addition, there is a knight on **f5**, but it is not threatening anything at the moment. White has a good move, e.g., 1. Qd1 - c2, to attack the knight on **f5** and to form a diagonal attack group against **h7**. Also, 1. Rf1 - e1 or 1. Bc1 -g5

is possible in order to finalize the development quickly. Unfortunately, White was a very careless player. He wanted to chase away the knight at **f5**. Therefore, he moved without thinking. **9**

1. g2 - g4?
As the official representative of the kings, I often receive complaints from kings from foreign countries. After the game, the White king at **g1** wrote to me to say that impudent players who senselessly ruin their own pawn line in front of their king should be forbidden from playing chess. My friend's furious outburst was only too understandable! Completely unnecessarily, White creates weak squares all around his own king. After all, almost every pawn move in front of your own king weakens your position. The pawn at **h3** is no longer defended by the g-pawn. The knight at **f3** has also lost a defender. If Black should build a diagonal attack group on the h2 - b8 diagonal using his queen and bishop, the g-pawn cannot move to **g3** to close the diagonal. Then,

1. ... Nf5 - h4
2. Bc1 - b2??
Here White had several possibilities to lose the game immediately. 2. Bc1 - g5? was not possible anymore because of 2. ... Nh4 x f3+ 3. Qd1 x f3 Qd8 x g5. Also, 2.Rf1 - e1? lost because of 2. ... Nh4 x f3+ 3. Qd1 x f3 Re8 x e1+.

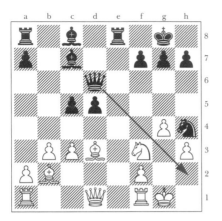

10 After 2. ... Qd8 - d6!: The White king has no hope.

The best move was the exchange on **h4** followed by Qd1 - f3. In any case, Black would keep the better options. With Bc1 – b2, White has removed his Black-square bishop from his king, instead of coming to his rescue. At least from **d2**, he would have been able to keep an eye on squares **e1**, **e3**, and **f4**. Instead, White moves him to a square where he cannot be effective at all. If White had not weakened himself with 1. g2 - g4?, then such a weak move would not be a catastrophe. But now, the end of the game is already decided.

2. ...   Qd8 - d6!   **10**

A simple trick: Now White cannot play 2. ...Nf4 x h4??, or 3. Qd6 - h2+ checkmate follows. On the other hand, 3. ... Nh4 x f3+ brings *4. Qd1 x f3 Qd6 - h2* is also checkmate. The White position is wide open, thanks to g2 - g4.

3. Rf1 - e1

This is White's only attempt to avoid checkmate. White can now move his king to **f1**.

3. ...   Re8 x e1+
4. Nf3 x e1

Unfortunately, this is necessary since 4. Qd1 x e1 does not work because of 4. ... Nh4 x f3+. Now, the path is clear for Black's diagonal attack.

4. ...   Qd6 - h2+
5. Kg1 - f1   Qh2 x h3+
6. Kf1 - g1

Or 6. Kf1 - e2 Bc8 x g4+, and Black will win further material with his next move.

6. ...   Bc7 - h2+
7. Kg1 - h1   Bh2 - g3+!

A discovered check. Black prepares the checkmate on **f2**.

8. Kh1 - g1   Qh3 - h2+
9. Kg1 - f1   Qh2 x f2 checkmate

Keep in mind that in chess, you need to have a reason for every move you make. Sometimes you may *need* to weaken your own king's position. This might be the case when, for example, you can gain a material advantage or attack the hostile king. However, without an important reason, you should never weaken your own position!

Game Strategies

In this chapter, we will examine six different types of games. Each is illustrated by a game played by a world champion. You shouldn't expect to understand all of the moves. Some of the ideas are so profound and deep that even master players need to study them for a long time to understand their meaning. Nevertheless, with the amount of knowledge you now have, you'll be able to understand the central themes of the individual games. And you'll find many tactical moves from the previous chapter in this one. Each of the following games uses a different opening. Simply watching how these master players move in this phase of the game will be helpful to you. You will realize how carefully good players work to dominate the center of the board. You will also see the considerable role development plays in chess. The importance of development is illustrated in game 1.

Opening Strategies

Game 1: Quick Development

At the start of a game, the following plan is very useful for a beginner. One or both of the central pawns (the e-pawn and the d-pawn) move forward two squares. This creates good possibilities for at least one of the bishops and helps establish a foothold for the pawn in the center. Then both knights and the king's bishop (White: bishop **f1**; Black: bishop **f8**) move out.

This development plan makes it possible for you to castle, moving your king to a position of maximum safety, before your opponent can begin an attack. For example, when your king stays on its initial square, your opponent might attack the weak square **f2** (Black: **f7**), because only the king is protecting it.

Game 1 shows the difference between a direct and uncompromising development strategy on the White side and a backward, old-fashioned development on the Black side. White can checkmate Black in only 17 moves.

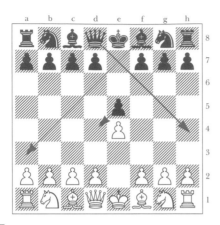

1 After 1. ... e7 - e5: Development and control of the center.

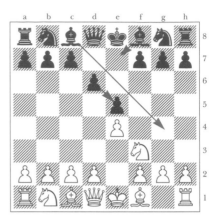

2 After 2. ... d7 - d6: Pawn e5 is guarded, but the development is neglected.

Paul Morphy, who was the first world champion in chess history, established a real chess monument with this game. From today's perspective, Black's opening moves are so bad that almost no player would use them. Nevertheless, the strength and the elegance with which Morphy wins the game are still a delight for chess lovers. By the way, this game is a favorite of a later world champion, Robert James "Bobby" Fischer.

**Paul Morphy (White) –
Duke of Braunschweig (Black),
Paris, 1858**

1. e2 - e4
This is still the most popular opening move. It presents the pos-sibility of bringing the bishop at **f1** into play, perhaps along with the queen. In addition, this move helps White dominate the center of the board.

After White moves the pawn into the center of the board, he would also like to move the neighboring pawn from **d2** to **d4**. Such a pawn duo in the center controls the fifth rank and prepares White to march forward later, perhaps to chase away hostile pieces. **1**

1. ...   e7 - e5
This move is simple and good. It also frees the Black bishop on **f8** and the queen. Black, too, wants to dominate the center of the board, and he is standing by in case of 2. d2 - d4 with 2. ... e5 x d4 to immediately demolish the White pawn duo.

2. Ng1 - f3
This is the most logical continuation. White develops his knight by moving him to an effective square. After only two moves, the first threat is apparent: *3. Nf3 x e5.* **2**

2. ...   d7 - d6

Black would have fewer problems if he defended his pawn at **e5** with 2. ... Nb8 - c6. The 2. ... d7 - d6 move does very little for Black's development because the important squares (**c5** and **b4**) are now blocked for the bishop on **f8**. We discussed this in the second example in "Checkmate in the First Few Moves." The rule of thumb for beginners is: In the first moves, try to move a central pawn forward with each move or to develop a minor piece so that you will be able to castle short as quickly as possible. You should not deviate from this rule unless you are faced with a special situation.

3. d2 - d4

White forms the pawn duo, and the bishop on **c1** is now free. Again, the pawn on **e5** is threatened with *4. d4 x e5   d6 x e5   5. Nf3 x e5.*

3. ...   Bc8 - g4?

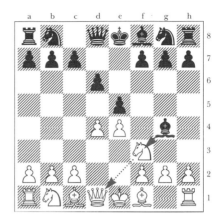

3 After 3. ... Bc8 - g4?: The knight at f3 is still pinned.

The Duke does not want to lose his central pawn foothold with 3. ...e5 x d4. However, he doesn't see that his move accelerates White's game development. At this point, besides capturing on **d4**, he can be more passive with 3. ... Nb8 - d7 (even though this locks in the bishop at **c8**) or move 3. ... Ng8 - f6, counter-attacking the pawn on **e4**.

The move 3. ... Bc8 - g4 pins the knight at **f3**. 4. d4 x e5 d6 x e5 5. Nf3 x e5 ?? is not possible because of 5. ... Q x d1 checkmate. But there is a mistake here.

4. d4 x e5   Bg4 x f3

Just in time, the Duke realizes that after 4. ... d6 x e5 5. Qd1 x d8+ Ke8 x d8, 6. Nf3 x e5 loses the e-pawn. After the exchange of queens, the knight pin at **f3** would no longer be valid. Therefore, Black must first exchange his bishop for the White knight on **f3** in order not to lose material.

5. Qd1 x f3   d6 x e5
6. Bf1 - c4   **4**

Here's another good development move. This one threatens checkmate on **f7**.

Earlier we pointed out that you should not rush the queen into the game too early. Here, the question is deceptive: Can you attack the queen now, or not? In diagram 4 (see next page), the queen on **f3** is active and safe. Due to his lead in development, White already has the advantage.

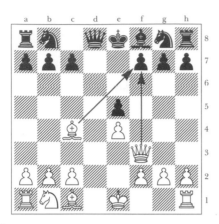

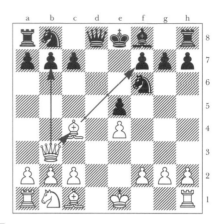

4 After 6. Bf1 - c4: Morphy threatens checkmate.

5 After 7. Qf3 - b3!: A double attack on b7 and f7.

6. ... Ng8 - f6?

Because this good development move is a mistake, it is clear that something is wrong with the Black position. 6. ... Qd8 - f6 was necessary, even though ideally **f6** is reserved for a knight. Nevertheless, Black should avoid the double attack.

7. Qf3 - b3!   **5**

With this move, White does not develop another piece and he does not castle, but he has a good reason for the move. The queen and bishop now form a diagonal attack group, and White threatens *8. Bc4 x f7+*. In addition, White threatens the pawn with *8. Qb3 x b7*. Black cannot ward off both threats at the same time. Still, he finds the best move in this miserable situation.

7. ... Qd8 - e7

This is a move to exchange the queens after 8. Qb3 x b7 with 8. ... Qe7 - b4+ (has an effect on **e1** and **b7**). Black will have to fight the endgame down one pawn, but at least he'll be able to finish developing his pieces. But the disadvantage of moving the queen is that the king's bishop on **f8** is now completely blocked. Therefore, Morphy decides to try his luck by further developing his pieces instead of playing an endgame.

8. Nb1 - c3!

This prevents the check on **b4**. Now White very strongly threatens with the *8. Qb3 x b7* move, and Black can no longer prevent the capture of his rook on **a8**.

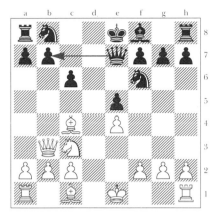

6 After 8. ... c7 - c6: When does the bishop on f8 get out?

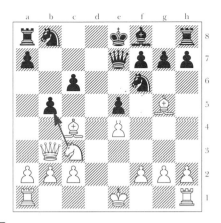

7 After 9. ... b7 - b5?: Before the demolition that follows the sacrifice.

8. ...   c7 - c6   **6**

Now the queen on **e7** guards the pawn on **b7**. But again, Black could not develop a piece, and he falls further behind in development.

9. Bc1 - g5

All of White's minor pieces are now out, but only one of Black's is. Because of this, White controls a much larger area of the board than his opponent does. With 9. Bc1 - g5, he pins the knight on **f6**. We cannot see a definite combination yet, but the confusion among the Black pieces leads us to assume that the Duke has to be very careful.

9. ...   b7 - b5?   **7**

9. ... Nb8 - d7 did not go well because of 10. Qb3 x b7 with a further attack on the rook on **a8** and the pawn on **c6**. But 9. ... Qe7 - c7 was necessary in order to finally devel-

op the other minor pieces. Understandably, the Duke wants to push back the annoying bishop at **c4**, and, at the same time, he wants to remove the pressure from the White queen against **b7**. But because his position is underdeveloped, the move of liberation, 9. ... b7 - b5?, becomes the key for Morphy's *dance of sacrifices*.

10. Nc3 x b5!

It starts! White is not willing to retreat. Instead, he uses a demolition sacrifice which allows him to direct all his pieces toward the Black king.

10. ...   c6 x b5
11. Bc4 x b5+   Nb8 - d7

Finally, Black is able to develop a piece, but the knight on **d7** is pinned, just like his colleague on **f6**. Morphy quickly increases the pressure:

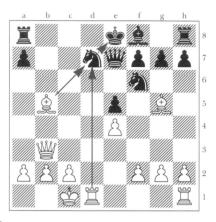

8 After 12. 0 - 0 - 0: The focal point is d7. Black is under pressure.

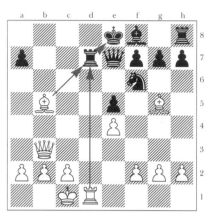

9 After 14. Rh1 - d1: All of White's pieces are active.

---

12. 0 - 0 - 0 **8**

This threatens *13. Bg5 x f6* followed by *14. Rd1 x d7* or *13. Rd1 x d7* right away (because the knight is pinned on **f6**). Even though other pieces are defending the knight on **d7**, Black would lose his queen if he fought back (discussed in the chapter "Attacking, Defending, and Removing Defensive Pieces").

12. ... Ra8 - d8

Black moves up another defender for **d7**. 12. ... 0 - 0 - 0? would lead to a quick end after 13. Bb5 - a6+ Kc8 - c7 14. Qb3 - b7 checkmate. Two of the protecting pawns on the seventh rank are simply missing.

13. Rd1 x d7!

Morphy has a simple reason for this move: His rook on **h1** is still waiting to get into the game. Because he sacrifices the rook at **d1**, White creates an opportunity to move his other

rook. Black, on the other hand, will not have an opportunity to activate his underdeveloped bishop at **f8** or his rook at **h8** because the queen on **e7** prevents all movement.

13. ... Rd8 x d7
14. Rh1 - d1 **9**

Again, the capture of the piece on **d7** is a threat to Black since he would have to give up his queen in the exchange of the pieces. Black now unpins his knight on **f6** and offers to exchange queens. Under the circumstances, this was the most promising move.

14. ... Qe7 - e6
15. Bb5 x d7+

Even though White could have a winning position with 15. Qb3 x e6+ f7 x e6 16. Bg5 x f6, followed by the capture on **d7**, he has a much faster and more elegant solution ready.

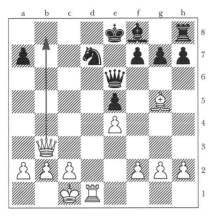

10 After 15. ... Nf6 x d7: Here's the masterpiece before the completion.

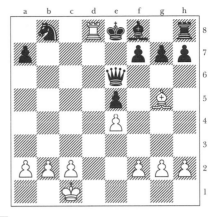

11 After 17. Rd1 - d8 checkmate: Queen, knight, rook sacrificed; but White wins.

---

15. ...   Nf6 x d7   **10**
16. Qb3 - b8+!!
This is called a diversion sacrifice. The knight on **d7** must now leave the d-file.

16. ...   Nd7 x b8
After he sacrifices his queen, White has only one bishop and one rook left for the attack, but that is enough to do the job.

17. Rd1 - d8 checkmate   **11**
In this game, Morphy gave his opponent a lesson in the matter of opening strategies. After only a few moves, Black had no way to move his king to safety with an early castle. He delayed the development of his pieces and, thus, gave his opponent the opportunity for a surprise attack. This is an impressive example of the kind of force taking the lead in development produces.

Middlegame Strategies

Game 2: Tactical Entanglements

Because of the possibilities for developing pieces, some opening systems seem to invite a search for tactical moves. This is especially true for the so-called gambit opening in which one side sacrifices a pawn in the hopes of receiving a lead in development or an advantage in position. Game 2 shows the former world champion Alekhine, playing as Black, fighting such a gambit opening. Alekhine did not believe in a passive defense. He preferred rejecting the sacrifice. An open-field battle develops. During this battle, one of Alekhine's knights "gets lost" in enemy territory. However, Alekhine's opponent cannot measure up to the tactical entanglements. He misses a good opportunity, and he finally fails because of the pointed counterattacks from the former world champion.

Games having complicated tactics naturally consist of numerous important variations and alternate ways to continue. In the remarks regarding many of these moves, you will find some analyses. Follow these in detail only if you are an especially talented and ambitious beginner. Should the variations seem confusing even after practice, you have the consolation of knowing that all chess players have strengths and weaknesses, even the world's top players. World champions Capablanca and Karpov made it all the way to the top without relying on the complex tactical moves that other players delight in displaying.

**Nyholm (White) –
Alexander Alekhine (Black),
Stockholm, 1912**

**1. e2 - e4   e7 - e5
2. d2 - d4**
This move is less popular than 2. Ng1 - f3 for a reason. After the simple answer…

2. …   e5 x d4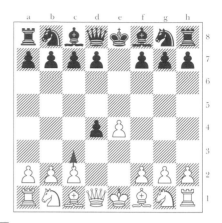

… it would not be helpful to counter by capturing the pawn with 3. Qd1 x d4 because, in doing so, White would neglect the development of his minor pieces. Even worse, after the natural answer 3. … Nb8 - c6, Black would attack the White queen. So White again could not develop a minor piece

12 **After 2. … e5 x d4: If White captures Qd1 x d4, then Nb8 - c6.**

because he would have to move his queen again. Therefore, White chooses another opening plan.

3. c2 - c3
White sacrifices a pawn in order to be able to develop his pieces quickly in case of 3. … d4 x c3 4. Nb1 x c3. Such an early pawn sacrifice is also called a gambit (from the Italian *gambio dare*, to trip someone up). From today's point of view, White's pawn sacrifice is playable. However, Black does not have much to worry about because he doesn't fall too far back in developing his pieces. Alekhine, though, foregoes the pawn gain and chooses instead a tactic which immediately creates an active game.

3. …   d7 - d5
In case of 4. c3 x d4, then 4. … d5 x e4, and Black has captured a pawn under favorable circumstances.

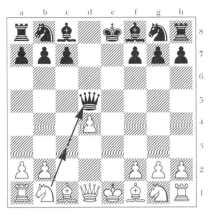

13 After 5. c3 x d4: Will White be able to chase away the Black queen?

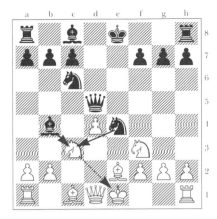

14 After 8. ... Nf6 - e4: The knight pinned at c3 becomes the object of an attack.

---

4. e4 x d5   Qd8 x d5
5. c3 x d4   **13**

White has reached equality in material, but like Black, he was not able to develop his pieces any further in the last two moves. White bases his hopes for an opening advantage on the position of the Black queen at **d5**. White will attack this queen and try to win a lead in development.

5. ...   Nb8 - c6

This develops the knight and attacks **d4**.

6. Ng1 - f3   Ng8 - f6
7. Bf1 - e2

7. Nb1-c3 was more consistent. Then Black would have answered with 7. ... Bf8 - b4 in order to pin the knight. But after the game-move, Black can take the initiative.

7. ...   Bf8 - b4+
8. Nb1 - c3   Nf6 - e4   **14**

This is the second attack on the knight pinned on **c3**.

9. Bc1 - d2

Nyholm defends the knight, unpins him, and threatens *10. Nc3 x d5*.

9. ...   Bb4 x c3

Alekhine does not want to lose any time moving his queen. Instead, he exchanges his bishop, in order to continue the development of his pieces.

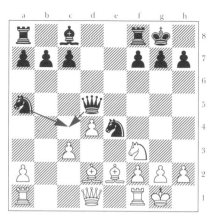

15 After 11. ... Nc6 - a5!: A fight for the square c4!

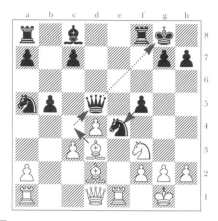

16 After 13. ... f7 - f5: This guards e4 but weakens the a2 - g8 diagonal.

10. b2 x c3   0 - 0
11. 0 - 0   Nc6 - a5!   15
Of course, the development of the only minor piece that has been inactive would be possible with 11. ... Bc8 - g4, but Alekhine views the position through the eyes of his opponent. What will White want to move next? At this point, the Black queen is dominating the center of the board. White would like to let his center pawns march forward in order to chase the queen away from **d5**. The move c3 - c4 seemed like a good idea.

With his move, Black prevents c3 - c4 and is ready to jump his knight to **c4**.

12. Rf1 - e1   b7 - b5
Here is another good move. It achieves several things at the same time. First, as a precaution, Black controls **c4**, so White's c-pawn cannot advance. At the same time, Black prepares a diag-

onal attack group on the a8 - h1 diagonal. If he also moves Bc8 - b7, then White must be very careful about moving his knight off **f3** because, if he does so, Black can move his knight away from **e4** onto any square and threaten *Qd5 x g2 checkmate*.

13. Be2 - d3
Now, White threatens the knight on **e4**.

13. ... f7 - f5   16
Black orientates his game toward controlling the light squares. He tries not to part with the squares **c4**, **e4**, and **d5**. But the move f7 - f5 also has a down side: The a2 - g8 diagonal is now open. Even though square **c4** is secure at the moment, Black will have to be careful about possible pins or checks on the a2 - g8 diagonal later.

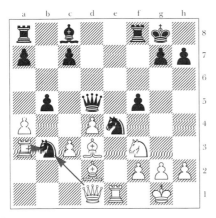

17 After 15. Ra1 - a3: The rook is aiming at the knight on b3.

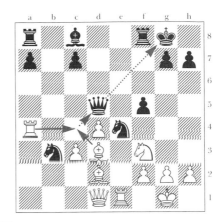

18 After 16. Ra3 x a4!: Careful! Bd3 - c4 threatens to pin the queen at d5.

14. a2 - a4!

After this, the real fun begins. White does not want to accept Black's domination of the light squares. Therefore, he wants to exchange the pawn at **b5** and at the same time increase the value of his a-pawn. But from **a2**, the a-pawn controls **b3**, an important invasion square. Now, Alekhine can occupy this square, in order to confuse the situation and finally win a pawn. In doing so, though, he risks his own neck, because White can pose all kinds of threats against his pieces.

14. ... Na5 - b3!

Guarded by the queen on **d5**, the knight threatens to win on the exchange with *15. ... Nb3 x a1*.

15. Ra1 - a3   **17**

The hunted becomes hunter! White threatens *16. Qd1 x b3* or *16. Ra3 x b3*.

15. ... b5 x a4

The capture on **a4** provides additional protection for the knight.

16. Ra3 x a4!   **18**

With *17. Bd3 - c4*, White would like to pin the Black queen in the next move and thus capture her. The rook on **a4** would cover the bishop.

16. ... Nb3 x d2

The exchange of the knight on **e4** with the bishop on **d2** prevents 17. Bd3 - c4, since this move would be followed by 17. ... Nd2 x c4. The bishop on **d2** guards the pawn on **c3**. For Black, the goal of the exchange is to remove the protection from the pawn at **c3** in order to capture him.

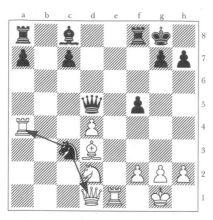

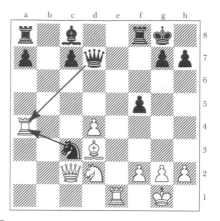

19 After 17. ... Ne4 x c3: A knight fork, but Bd3 - c4 is still a possibility.

20 After 18. ... Qd5 - d7!: The queen flees to d7 and attacks the rook on a4.

17. Nf3 x d2   Ne4 x c3   **19**

Success! The pawn is captured, but note that the knight on **c3** provides a fork, attacking the queen on **d1** and the rook on **a4**. The pin move, Bd3 - c4, is still possible. Now, however, if White should counter with 18. Bd3 - c4, Black would play 18. ... Qd5 x c4, fol-lowed by 19. ... Nc3 x d1 and then have one more pawn in the end-game.

18. Qd1 - c2?

As you follow the variations to move 24, try to develop a feeling for how complicated tactical entanglements can be. With this move, White is threat-ening with *19. Qc2 x c3* and *19. Bd3 - c4*. Unfortunately, Nyholm does not look far enough ahead. With 18. Qd1 - a1!, he would have avoided the fol-lowing development. The threat would then have been the pin, *19. Bd3 - c4* with the gain of the queen and

19. Qa1 x c3 with the gain of the knight. If Black had then countered with 18. ...Qd5 - d7, in order to secure his queen and at the same time to threaten *19. ... Qd7 x a4*, then 19. Ra4 x a7   Ra8 x a7   20. Qa1 x a7 would have been possible, winning back the pawn and, important, guarding the pawn on **d4**. Instead of 18. ... Qd5 - d7, Alekhine would have sacrificed the queen through 18. ... Nc3 x a4 19. Bd3 - c4   Qd5 x c4 (or 19. ... Na4 - b6)   20. Nd2 x c4 Na4 - b6. The rook/bishop/pawn for queen exchange creates a very complicated situation. The difference between 18. Qd1 - c2 and 18. Qd1 - a1 is that the latter move also threatens the **a7** pawn.   **20**

18. ...   Qd5 - d7!

Alekhine prevents a queen pin with 19. Bd3 - c4 and also attacks the White rook on **a4.** Now 19. Qc2 x c3 would be countered with 19. ...Qd7 x a4.

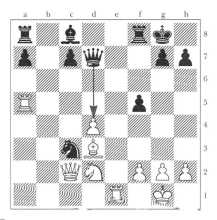

21 After 19. Ra4 - a5?: The pawn on d4 is unguarded.

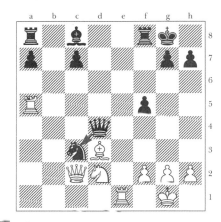

22 After 19. ... Qd7 x d4!: Black captures d4 and guards the knight on c3.

19. Ra1 - a5? **21**

With 19. Bd3 - c4+, White still would have stayed in the game. After 19. ... Nc3 - d5, 20. Bc4 x d5+ Qd7 x d5 21. Qc2 x c7 would have followed, winning back the pawn, and 19. ... Kg8 - h8 could have been answered with 20. Ra4 - a3. White hopes to block the retreat of the knight on **c3**. But Alekhine has calculated more precisely.

19. ... Qd7 x d4! **22**

19. ... Nc3 - d5 would have been a very bad move because of 20. Ra5 x d5 Qd7 x d5 21. Bd3 - c4. Also 19. ... Nc3 - e4 was not good because of 20. Nd2 x e4 f5 x e4 21. Bd3 x e4 (an attack on the rook on **a8**) 21. ... Ra8 - b8 22. Be4 x h7+ Kg8 - h8 23. Ra5 - h5. At the end, White would keep one pawn more, and the possibility of attacking the king. This move secures the knight on **c3**. Alekhine, though, had already calculated his answer to White's next move.

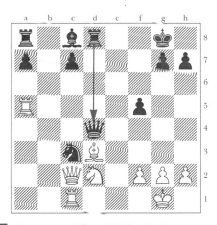

23 After 20. ... Rf8 - d8!: The Black attack group in the d-file threatens square d3.

20. Re1 - c1

Again the **c3** knight is "hung up," threatened by 21. Qc2 x c3.

20. ... Rf8 - d8! **23**

In order to answer 21. Qc2 x c3 with 21. ... Qd4 x d3.

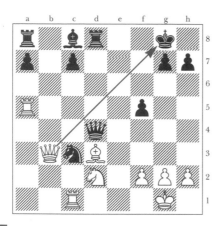

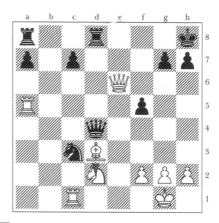

24 After 21. Qc2 - b3+, a tricky check: White is threatening Rc1 x c3.

25 After 22. ... Kg8 - h8: Now, if the bishop moves, the knight falls.

---

21. Qc2 - b3+　　　　**24**

This is what White had counted on with 19. Ra4 - a5. In case of 21. + Kg8 - h8, then 22. Rc1 x c3 wins one piece as the bishop on **d3** would then be guarded. After 21. ... Nc3 - d5 comes the rapid transaction 22. Nd2 - f3 (an attack on the queen) 22. ... Qd4 - f4 (an attack on the rook on **c1**) 23. ... Ra5 x d5! Qf4 x c1+. 24. Bd3 - f1 Bc8 - e6 (a discovered check by the rook on **d5** was threatened, and after 24. ... Rd8 x d5 and 25. Qb3 x d5+ Kg8 - h8 comes 26. Qd5 x a8) 25. Rd5 x d8+ Ra8 x d8 26. Qb3 x e6+ Kg8 - h8 27. Nf3 - e5 presents a winning position for White.

21. ... Bc8 - e6!!

A bishop sacrifice secures the advantage. White will lose a d-file piece.

22. Qb3 x e6+

Or 22. Qb3 x c3 Qd4 x d3 with two pawns more and a winning position.

22. ... Kg8 - h8　　　　**25**

23. Ra5 - e5?

23. Bd3 x f5 Qd4 x d2 would not be good, and now 24. Rc1 - a1 Rd8 - e8 loses, as well as 24. Rc1 - e1 Nc3 - e2+ ! 25. Re1 x e2 Qc3 x a5. But White should have tried 23. Ra5 - a3. After 23. ... Qd5 x d3 24. Ra3 x c3 Qd3 x d2 25. Rc3 x c7, the victory would still have been difficult. Notice that 25. ... Qd2 - d1+ would not lead to checkmate because of 26. Qe6 - e1.

23. ... Qd4 x d3

24. Rc1 - e1　　　　**26**

White is still hoping to outwit the opponent with a checkmate on the eighth rank. So Alekhine creates some breathing room for himself:

24. ... h7 - h6

Of course not 24. ...Qd3 x d2 25. Qe6 - e8+! Rd8 x e8 26. Re5 x e8 Ra8 x e8 27. Re1 x e8 checkmate.

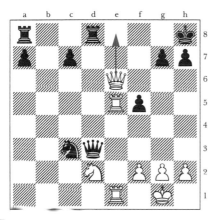

26 After 24. Rc1 - e1: Be careful of a checkmate on the eighth rank!

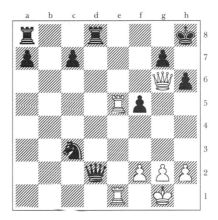

27 27 After 25. ... Qd3 x d2: Chess blindness! White has lost the knight on d2.

25. Qe6 - g6?

This is chess blindness. During the course of the game, White obviously lost his balance. Here, he overlooks the fact that Black can simply capture the knight on **d2**. Down two rooks and with no possible way to attack, Nyholm was lost anyway.

25. ...   Qd3 x d2   **27**
26. resigns

With 26. Re5 - e8+ Rd8 x e8 27. Re1 x e8+ Ra8 x e8 28. Qg6 x e8+ Kg8 - h7, White can still get in a few revenge checks, but because of the breathing room on **h7**, there will be no checkmate. The material superiority would allow Alekhine an easy victory, so White decides that it's no use to continue.

Game 3: Game on the Queen's Side

In this game you will see that there are plans which at first have almost nothing to do with the hostile king. In the following game, White wins by attacking on the a - c files; in other words, on the queen's side. He does this even though both parties have castled short. White succeeds in penetrating the Black position and finally in capturing an important pawn. Such games are essentially calmer than the previous example. The strategy demands long-range planning. In the end though, tactics play a role. In this game in which former world champion Petrosian is playing White, tactics help him realize an overwhelming advantage in position.

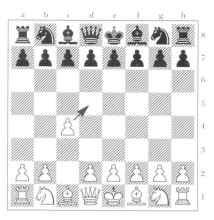

28 After 1. c2 - c4: This is known as the English opening.

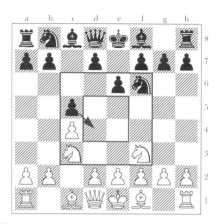

29 29 After 3. ... c7 - c5: These squares form central core and expanded center.

**Tigran Petrosian (White) –
Lev Psakhis (Black),
Las Palmas, 1982**

1. c2 - c4   **28**

Not all master games proceed according to a perfect development scheme, as we've seen in the first two games. Petrosian was among those players who liked to hold back their central pawns in their opening moves, bringing them into action somewhat later. When you pay close attention, this strategy is fine, but you must be careful that you develop your pieces at the right moment. 1. c2 - c4 is known as the English opening.

1. ...   Ng8 - f6

Developing the knight is a natural, good move.

2. Nb1 - c3

Already you see the difference between this and the previous games. Neither side can attack hostile pawns after the first moves. Each develops his position more or less independent of the moves of the opponent—but don't be fooled. Sooner or later, there will be enemy contact.

2. ...   e7 - e6

This move may prepare the way for d7 - d5. It also opens up development possibilities for the bishop on **f8**.

3. Ng1 - f3   c7 - c5   **29**

Psakhis is not willing to leave the center to his opponent. He wants to have a foothold in the center of the board. To accomplish this, 3. ... d7 - d5 was also a good possibility.

Since there are few contacts or possibilities to capture in this position, the idea of development is not so decisive here. However, control of the center of the board is very important.

We call squares **d4**, **e4**, **d5**, and **e5** the central core, and the adjacent squares form the expanded center (see diagram 29).

Maybe in the beginning, you won't understand why the squares in the center of the board are more important than the squares along the edges. You must realize that pieces in the center, especially knights, have a much bigger effect on the game than those on the edge because they can quickly reach squares on both sides. This is somewhat similar to a tennis player or a badminton player who automatically moves back to the center of the court after each shot because from there he can quickly reach every possible spot on the court.

The idea is the same in chess. When both sides place mostly pawns in the center or the expanded center, their strategy is to deny some center squares to hostile pieces. In the long run, their pawns may be pushed further, to hunt other pieces. Additionally, the presence of their pawns immediately creates a central foothold that will protect any of their own pieces moved into the area.

4. g2 - g3

This is how Petrosian liked to play. He wants to develop his king's bishop toward **g2** and the long h1 - a8 diagonal. Chess players call this development a *fianchetto*. As you can see, such a *fianchetto* on **g2** is well suited to support an attack on the hostile queen's side.

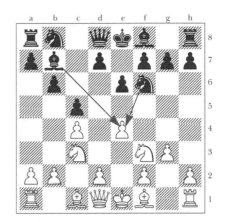

30 After 5. ... Bc8 - b7: The pawn on e4 comes under attack.

4. ...   b7 - b6

Black doesn't want to give up the long h1 - h8 diagonal without a fight. Therefore, he makes a *fianchetto* with his White-square bishop.

5. e2 - e4

Suddenly, the e-pawn appears on **e4**! 5. Bf1 - g2 would have been normal, but with his opponent not yet fully developed, Petrosian wants to increase his influence in the center. Even though the **e4** pawn is attacked by the knight on **f6**, he is sufficiently defended by the knight on **c3**.

5. ...   Bc8 - b7   **30**

Another attack on the **e4** pawn.

6. Qd1 - e2

The queen guards **e4**. The position becomes unusual, and, thus, is typical of Tigran Petrosian. In contrast to game 1, diagram 6, here the queen is

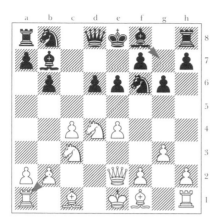

31 After 8 ... g7 - g6?: A questionable *fianchetto*, d6 will lose protection.

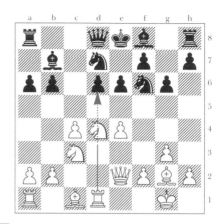

32 After 12. Rf1 - d1!: The rook on d1 will attack d6 later.

not in the way of her own bishop. He will be developed on the "long diagonal." The advance, 6. e4 - e5, was still too risky here, because after 6. ... Nf6 - g4, the pawn at **e5** comes under attack. The knight at **f3** would be pinned by the bishop on **b7**.

6. ...   d7 - d6?
Better 6. ... Nb8 - c6 as a development move, to prevent the White pawns from marching up the center.

7. d2 - d4
This threatens to confine the opponent even more with *8. d4 - d5*.

7. ...   c5 x d4
8. Nf3 x d4   g7 - g6?   **31**
Now, Black uses a *fianchetto* with his second bishop. The problem is the pawn on **d6**. Black exchanged his c-pawn already. His e-pawn has advanced to **e6**. Now, the pawn on **d6**

has no protection from other pawns. At this point, Psakhis, too, wants to remove his bishop from the protection of the d-pawn. But this will lead to problems in the latter stages of the game since Petrosian is capable of directing his pieces against **d6**.

9. Bf1 - g2   a7 - a6
Without this move, Black would always have to expect *Nd4 - b5*, an attack on the Black pawn at **d6**.

10. 0 - 0   Nb8 - d7
11. Rf1 - d1!   **32**
Rooks belong on files not blocked by their own pawns. Petrosian's rook on **d1** already toys with the pawn on **d6**, which is not guarded at this time. Even though the knight on **d4** is temporarily between the rook and the pawn, the rook is in the right place, and, at the appropriate time, the knight will get out of the rook's way.

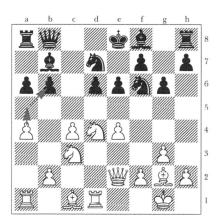

33 After 12. a2 a4!: The a pawn initiates the attack.

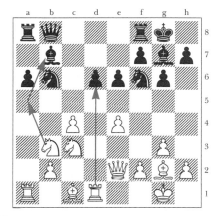

34 After 15. Nd4 - b3!: The knight moves to a5; the d1 rook is now in the clear

11. ... Qd8 - b8

As a precaution, Psakhis uses his queen to defend the pawn on **d6** before he removes the king's bishop from the a3 - f8 diagonal. Having your own queen on the same file as a hostile rook isn't a pleasant experience. This situation can easily become a pin, because the Black queen is lost if all the pieces between the rook and queen would move away.

12. a2 - a4!   **33**

White begins the attack on the queen's side. The goal of the pawn advance is to open the a-file with *a4 - a5, a5 x b6,* and then to direct the rook at **a1** against the pawn on **a6**. In addition, this will free square **a5**, still controlled by the pawn on **b6**, for a White knight. The following part of the game shows what Petrosian has in mind because here he succeeds in realizing almost all of his goals.

12. ... Bf8 - g7
13. a4 - a5   0 - 0

Black was able to finalize the development, but his position is confined. He has no prospect for an active game since his pieces are too far from the White camp.

14. a5 x b6   Nd7 x b6
15. Nd4 - b3!   **34**

Petrosian would prefer to make the bishop on **g2** a partner in the attack. Now, he maneuvers his knight from **d4** via **b3** to **a5** to exchange the knight for the bishop on **b7**. Then, possibly, he will try to open the long diagonal for the bishop with *e4 - e5.* This move also unblocks the rook on **d1** so that he can attack **d6**.

15. ... Ra8 - a7

Psakhis must maneuver in a tight space. As a precaution, he moves his rook out of the long diagonal.

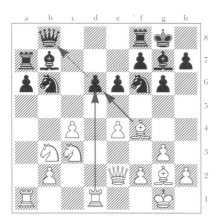

35 After 16. Bc1 - f4!: The pawn on d6 is really under attack!

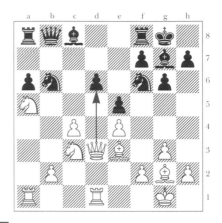

36 After 19. Qe2 - d3: A new attack on d6.

---

16. Bc1 - f4!   **35**

Now, the pawn on **d6** is pinned and being attacked by two pieces. Black sees no good way to protect him. Therefore, he decides to move his e-pawn forward. But that gives White new opportunities.

16. ...   e6 - e5

Each pawn move weakens at least one square, so be careful with your pawn moves! Too often players wish they could move a pawn back, but that is never possible. Even though 16. ... e6 - e5 prevents the possibility that White will later open the long h1 - a8 diagonal with his own *e4 - e5*, the e-pawn gives up his control of square **d5**. Seven moves later, one of Petrosian's knights will appear there and force a decisive opening. The defensive move, 16. ... Rf8 - d8, would have made 17. c4 - c5 possible because the pawn on **d6** is pinned.

17. Bf4 - e3   Bb7 - c8

With the retreat of the bishop, Black guards the knight on **b6** with his queen. At the same time, the White-square bishop flees from the knight on **b3**, who would like to exchange him after *Nb3 - a5*. Even though White cannot now open up the long diagonal (the pawn on **e5** blocks the White e-pawn), the pawn on **a6** would lose a covering piece in the exchange of the bishop **b7**. And in the following moves, the pawn at **a6** is Petrosian's actual goal.

18. Nb3 - a5

Now, the rook on **a7** and the queen on **b8** are threatened with a knight fork with *Na5 - c6*.

18. ...   Ra7 - a8
19. Qe2 - d3   **36**

Another move aimed at the pawn on **d6**. Have a look at the bishop on **g7**.

Game Strategies

90

If he were standing on **e7**, Black would have no problem guarding the pawn on **d6**. Even worse, the move, e6 - e5, blocks in the bishop on **g7**. He has no chance to attack the White queen's side (c3 - a1) because his own e-pawn blocks his movement.

19. ... Bc8 - e6

Here's a counterattack on the pawn on **c4**. After 20. Qd3 x d6, 20. ... Nb6 x c4, 21. Na5 x c4 Be6 x c4 and Black holds out. Also with 20. Be3 x b6 Qb8 x b6 21. Qd3 x d6 Qb6 x b2, White does not gain any material advantage. Therefore, Petrosian continues to play calmly for the time being. He covers the pawn on **c4** in order to renew the threat 20. Qd3 x d6.

20. b2 - b3   Nb6 - c8

Not a good move with the knight on the eighth rank in the way of the Black rooks. He can only influence a few squares, and he has no chance to play an active role. But Black must somehow cover the d-pawn, and 20. ... Rf8 - d8 was not possible because of the knight fork after 21. Na5 - c6. His opening strategy has failed. The next move is typical of Petrosian. White realizes that he has his opponent under control and that he can maneuver very deliberately.

21. h2 - h3

In an open-field battle, such a loss of time would be unforgivable. Here, however, Black has no counterplay. He cannot mount a threat so, as a precaution, White secures square **g4**.

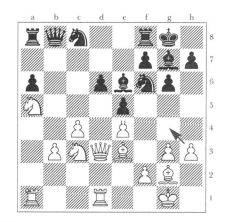

37 After 21. h2 - h3: White has total control, Black is without counterplay

He has time now for such "amenities" because his pieces are standing so well that the opponent can hardly improve his position.

22. ... h7 - h5

This is not the start of an attack. Black has too few forces on the king's side. You almost always need to have more attackers than defenders in order to mount a successful attack. Actually, 22. ... h7 - h5 is an uneasy move. Black hopes that at one point he can move his bishop to **h6** if the bishop on **e3** moves away.

22. b3 - b4!

The queen's side advance continues.

22. ... Qb8 - c7

Black does not have a move that really makes sense. On 22. ... Qb6 x b4, 23. Rd1 - b1 traps the queen. Still, Psakhis increases the pressure on the pawn on

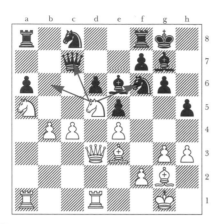

38 After 23. Nc3 - d5: As a result of e6 - e5, the knight on c3 gets to d5.

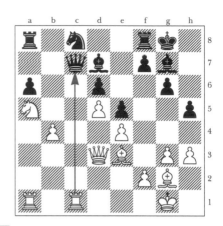

39 After 25. Rd1 - c1: White occupies the open c-file.

c4 with 22. ... Qb8 - c7, even though the pawn is still guarded by the knight on **a5** and the queen on **d3**.

23. Nc3 - d5   **38**

White's move interrupts the attack line of the bishop on **e6** against the pawn on **c4**, and, at the same time, it attacks the Black queen. It was e6 - e5 (Black's 16th move) which made it possible for the knight to move to **d5**.

23. ...   Nf6 x d5

The knight on **d5** is simply too powerful. Psakhis must exchange it.

24. c4 x d5

Now the c-file is free of pawns. Obviously, the Black rooks cannot get to the c-file as fast as the White ones can, since Black's own knight is in his way on **c8**. Also, the Black queen is not well positioned on **c7**. As soon as a White rook appears in the c-file, she

will have to flee. For now, the bishop on **e6** is threatened and must move.

24. ...   Be6 - d7
25. Rd1 - c1   **39**

The rook has done a good job for White on the d-file. He helped force the pawn move, e6 - e5, which made the knight move, Nc3 - d5, possible. Now, the rook on **d1** is blocked by his own pawn on **d5**. He can no longer attack on the d-file, so moves to the open c-file to attack the Black queen.

25. ...   Qc7 - b8

It is even simpler for White with 25. ... Qc7 - d8 26. Na5 - c6 (threatens 26. Nc6 x d8 and 26. Ra1 x a6) 26. ... Bd7 x c6 Rc1 x c6, and the pawn on **a6** falls without Black receiving anything in exchange.

26. Na5 - c6   Qb8 - b7

After 26. ... Bd7 x c6 27. d5 x c6

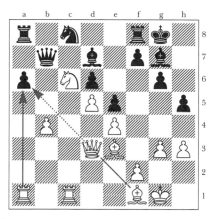

40 After 26. ... Bg2 - f1: The goal of a6 is now in sight.

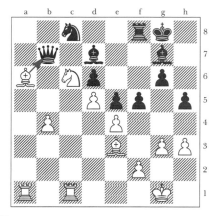

41 After 29. Bf1 x a6: The Black queen cannot escape.

Qb8 x b4?, 28. Rc1 - b1! is possible. The Black queen then has no square and is lost. Even worse would be 26. ... Qb8 c7?? because of 27. Nc6 - e7+ Kg8 - h8 28. Rc1 x c7.

27. Bg2 - f1!

Petrosian is getting serious. He decides to capture the pawn on **a6,** so moves his bishop to the f1 - a6 diagonal.

27. ... f7 - f5   40

Throughout the game, Psakhis has been depressed, because he never had a real countergame. Now, he wants to activate his pieces and pawns on the king's side to start an attack there; but it is too late. White is getting ready to make his decisive move.

28. Qd3 x a6!

A surprising tactical move in a game that has been strictly strategic to now. The White queen sacrifices herself,

but Petrosian has calculated that he will also capture the hostile queen and, in the end, maintain an advantage in pieces. Notice that 28. Ra1 x a6? was not a good idea because of the in-between move, 28. ... f5 x e4!, with its attack on the White queen. In case of 29. Qd3 x e4?, then 29. ... Ra8 x a6 30. Bf1 x a6 Qb7 x a6, and Black has won one bishop.

28. ... Ra8 x a6   41
29. Bf1 x a6

When you look closely, you can see that the Black queen cannot escape now. After 29. ... Qb7 - a8, 30. Ba6 x c8 (the rook on **a1** attacks the queen on **a8**) follows, and 30. ... Qa8 x c8 31. Nc6 - e7+ (a knight fork) 31. ... Kg8 - h8 32. Ne7 x c8. White continues to have one more pawn and the exchange. 29. ... Qb7 - c7 30. Nc6 - e7+ Kg8 - h8 31. Rc1 x c7 is even more hopeless, and White has

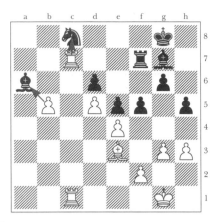

42 After 33. b4 - b5!: Black loses the bishop on a6 or the knight on c8.

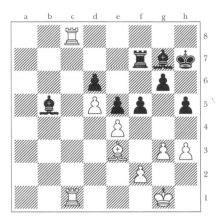

43 After 34. ... Kg8 - h7: White wins more material.

one more rook. Upon moving to any other square, the queen would be lost immediately. So Black decides to move her out voluntarily.

29. ... Bd7 x c6
30. Ba6 x b7 Bc6 x b7

Until now, Black was materially even. He has won two minor pieces for the rook and pawn. But White's attack on the queen's side is not yet finished, and he inevitably wins more material.

31. Rc1 - c7

Here, White threatens the bishop on **b7**. Black has only one defense

31. ... Rf8 - f7
32. Ra1 - c1

White threatens to win one bishop with *33. Rc7 x f7 Kg8 x f7 34. Rc1 - c7+ Kf7 - g8 35. Rc7 x b7*. Black makes the only possible move and, for the time being, saves the bishop.

33. ... Bb7 - a6
33. b4 - b5!   **42**

This is White's diversion sacrifice. The bishop on **a6** covers the knight on **c8**. White now threatens *34. b5 x a6*. Psakhis must capture the pawn on **b5** and give up the protection of the knight.

33. ... Ba6 x b5
34. Rc7 x c8+ Kg8 - h7   **43**

Black resigns at the same time. Playing against a world champion down one on Exchange in the endgame is hopeless, unless there is some kind of compensation. A possible continuation would be:

35. Rc1 - c7   Rf7 x c7
36. Rc8 x c7   f5 x e4
37. Be3 - g5

This move threatens to exploit the pin of the bishop on **g7** with *38. Bg5 - f6*.

37. ... Kh7 - g8
38. Bg5 - e7

Now, Black cannot save the pawn on d6 since White would answer 38. ... Bg7 - f8 with 39. Rc7 - c8 and capture the bishop.

38. ... Bb5 - a4
39. Be7 x d6   Ba4 - b3

An attempt to capture the pawn on **d5**.

40. Rc7 - d7!

Although 40. Rc7 - c5 is possible, the rook can be more helpful on **d7**.

41. ... Bb3 x d5
41. Bd6 x e5!   Bg7 x e5
42. Rd7 x d5

In this simplified position (neither side has many pieces), the superior rook will, in collaboration with the king, quickly capture one or two Black pawns. After that, White will march one of his pawns onto the eighth rank and promote him to a queen. Checkmate is then only a matter of time.

Game 4: Pawn Assault against the King

In most games, both parties castle short within ten to fifteen moves to quickly ensure the safety of their kings. In order to castle short, you only have to move two pieces, the bishop on **f1** and the knight on **g1**. For castling long, you must move the knight on **b1**, the bishop on **c1**, and the queen on **d1**.

Games are especially interesting when one side castles short and the other castles long. In these games, both sides can attack the opponent's kingside with pawns without weakening their own king position. The goal of advancing the pawns is to chase away the opponent's defensive pieces, to demolish the opponent's pawn position, and, above all, to open the files for one's own rooks. In the following game, Bobby Fischer shows how this works. Speaking of the attack scheme which he uses in this game, he once said, "Such positions almost play themselves. One opens the h-line, sacrifices some pieces and then the mate comes along." His opponent, the strong master Bent Larsen, has his own attack plans against Fischer's king. But when one side castles short, and one long, it is a matter of whose attack goes through faster. And in this game, Fischer's attack is the faster one, even though by only one move.

Fischer (White) – Larsen (Black), Portoroz, 1958

1. e2 - e4   c7 - c5

Black chooses the Sicilian Defense. The move 1. ... c7 - c5 achieves very little for the development of the Black minor pieces. However, the pawn on **c5** controls the central square **d4**, and Black decides later which square his central pawns on the d-file and e-file will move to. The Sicilian Defense is an aggressive and very popular opening system. But

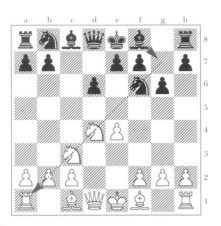

44 After 5. ... g7 - g6: The bishop turns into a dragon.

precisely because Black neglects his development to some extent, it is a very dangerous opening for beginners.

2. Ng1 - f3   d7 - d6

Again Larsen's move achieves relatively little for his own development. Still, the pawn on **d6** controls the central square **e5**. Thus, Black will soon be able to move a knight to **f6** without risking having the knight chased away by e4 - e5.

3. d2 - d4

White advances in the center and offers to exchange pawns, allowing him to develop both bishops quickly.

3. ...   c5 x d4
4. Nf3 x d4   Ng8 - f6

This attacks the pawn on **e4**. In the following moves, Black tries to quickly develop the pieces on his king's side, especially the bishop on **f8**.

5. Nb1 - c3   g7 - g6   **44**

Larsen uses a *fianchetto* for his king's bishop. This is called the Dragon Variation of the Sicilian Defense. The bishop on **f8** has an interesting diagonal in the direction of **a1** from **g7**. In many games, the bishop rages like a fire-breathing dragon on this long diagonal. However, this game plan is also rather dangerous for Black, as you will see.

6. Bc1 - e3

Fischer indicates that he wants to castle long in order to stage a pawn attack on the king's side. Otherwise, he would have played 6. Bf1 - e2, in order to prepare for castling short.

6. ...   Bf8 - g7
7. f2 - f3

This is an important move. As a precaution, White defends the central pawn on **e4** again. This move also serves as a preparation for g2 - g4, to chase away the defending knight on **f6** with a further *g4 - g5*. Finally, 7. f2 - f3 prevents Black from using Nf6 - g4 to exchange the bishop on **e3**. White has plans for the bishop on **e3**.

7. ...   0 - 0
8. Qd1 - d2   Nb8 - c6
9. Bf1 - c4   Nc6 x d4

Larsen wants to move his bishop from **c8** to **e6** to fight Fischer's bishop for control of the a2 - g8 diagonal. Playing 9. ... Bc8 - e6 immediately would have failed because of 10. Bc4 x e6 f7 x e6 11. Nd4 x e6.

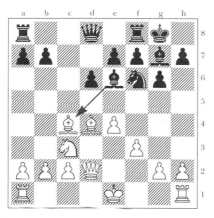

45 After 10. ... Bc8 - e6: Should White exchange on e6?

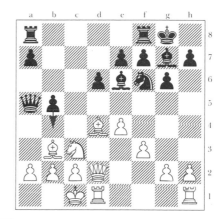

46 After 12. ... b7 - b5: The first assault from a Black pawn.

10. Be3 x d4   Bc8 - e6   **45**

In games between masters, the fight is often about dominating the individual central squares. If Fischer had played <u>11. Bc4 x e6   f7 x e6,</u> the pawn front around the Black king would have become a little crumbly. However, the new e-pawn on **e6** would have controlled **d5** and thus prevented Nc3 - d5. This is why Fischer prefers to move the unguarded bishop from **c4** to the safety of **b3**.

11. Bc4 - b3   Qd8 - a5

From here, the Black queen can support the advance b7 - b5, which would not be possible immediately because of *12. Nc3 x b5*.

12. 0 - 0 - 0   b7 - b5   **46**

White has castled long, and Black has castled short. In games like this, the pawns often hurry forward toward the hostile king. Here, the b-pawn will move forward to **b4** to chase Fischer's defending knight away from **c3** and to increase the chances for a successful attack against the White king.

13. Kc1 - b1

Fischer already sees that his opponent will set up his rooks in the c-file because the c-file is partially open. This means that only one White pawn is in the way of the Black rooks. Files that are partially open can be just as valuable as open lines. After all, it is most important that their own pawns not hamper the rooks.

In order to avoid a pin later on, the White king uses this relatively quiet moment to flee out of the dangerous c-file. Later, when both sides really start to attack, the time may be too late for such security precautions.

13. ... b5 - b4

14. Nc3 - d5   Be6 x d5

As in the previous game, the White knight is so strong on **d5** that Larsen prefers to exchange him immediately.

15. Bb3 x d5   Ra8 - c8?

Later, he discovered that the rook on **a8** should have stayed in his place to support the advance of the a-pawn. Instead, Larsen should have exchanged with 15. ... Nf6 x d5.

16. Bd5 - b3

Now, Fischer can keep this important bishop. He not only presses on **f7**, he also defends the pawns on **a2** and **c2**.

16. ... Rc8 - c7

Larsen wants to double his rooks in the c-file to develop more pressure on **c2**. In addition, the pawn on **a7** is now guarded, so the Black queen can move without allowing the bishop on **d4** to capture the a-pawn.

17. h2 - h4   **47**

Only now does Fischer begin his pawn assault. His goal is to open the h-file so that he can attack there with his rooks and queen. The pawn on **g6** offers him an attack point at **h5**. If the h-pawn can move forward to **h5**, he can open the h-file with h5 x g6, bringing the rook on **h1** into play.

17. ... Qa5 - b5

Larsen wants to move his a-pawn to **a4** to press the bishop on **b3** and then

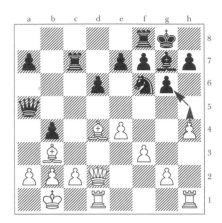

47 After 17. h2 - h4: The beginning of White's pawn assault on the h-file.

to demolish the front of White's pawn line on the queen's side.

18. h4 - h5

Fischer accelerates the speed of his attack! He offers a pawn sacrifice. An analysis of the complicated consequences of accepting this sacrifice would be too much at this point. We'll only show the following variation here as an example: 18. ... Nf6 x h5 19. Bd4 x g7 Kg8 x g7 20. g2 - g4 Nh5-f6 21. Qd2 - h6+ Kg7 - g8 22. g4 - g5 Nf6 - h5 23. Rh1 x h5! g6 x h5 24. g5 - g6 h7 x g6 25. Qh6 x g6+ Kg8 - h8 26. Qg6 - h6+ Kh8 - g8 27. Rd1 - g1+ Qa5 - g5 28. Rg1 x g5 checkmate.

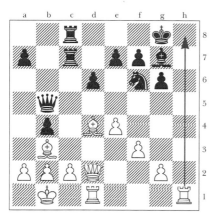

48 After 19. ... h7 x g6: This opens the line for the major pieces.

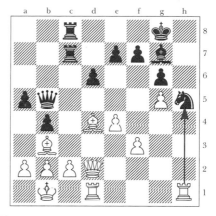

49 After 21. ... Nf6 - h5: White will sacrifice the Exchange.

18. ...   Rf8 - c8
19. h5 x g6   h7 x g648   **48**

Done! The White rook on **h1** has a clear path on the h-file and can now be used against the Black king.

20. g2 - g4

White brings the g-pawn into the game to chase away the knight on **f6**.

20. ...   a7 - a5

Black follows his own plans. If he could play a5 - a4 in time, White would have problems. But from this point on, Fischer controls the action.

21. g4 - g5   Nf6 - h5   **49**

22. Rf1 x h5!

Here's a sacrifice of the Exchange! It also serves to demolish the line of Black pawns. The Black pawn on **g6** must leave his place so that his White colleague can advance to this square.

22. ...   g6 x h5
23. g5 - g6   **50**

In the diagram on page 100, pay attention to the bishop on **b3**. He is pinning the pawn on **f7**. The bishop on **b3** and the pawn on **g6** now work together. Next, White will be able to open up the g-file for his rook and queen.

23. ...   e7 - e5

Also after 23. ...e7 - e6   24. g6 x f7+ Kg8 x f7 (or 24. ... Rc7 x f7   25. Bb3 x e6)   25. Bd4 x g7   Kg8 x g7   26. Rd1 - g1+   Kg7 - h7   27. Qd2 - g2, the Black king is vulnerable to attack from the White pieces.

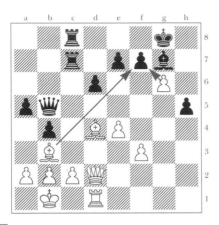

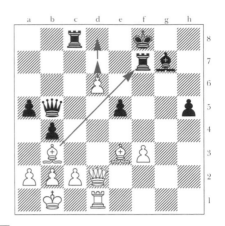

50 After 23. g5 - g6: The focal point is the square f7.

51 After 25. d5 - d6: The free pawn runs.

24. g6 x f7+ Kg8 - f8
25. Bd4 - e3
Sometimes, it is not as important what square a piece moves to as which square it leaves! The main idea of this move is *26. Qd2 x d6+*.

25. ... d6 - d5
This sacrifice wards off the threat from *26. Qd2 x d6*, and, at the same time, it strips the protection of the bishop on **b3** from the pawn on **f7**.

26. e4 x d5   Rc7 x f7
27. d5 - d6   **51**
Fischer uses his free pawn. The pawn threatens to march straight up to **d8** and be promoted to a queen. If he reaches square **d7**, then he renews the

threat of bringing the White queen into the attack with Qd2 - d6+. In addition, of course, he also threatens to win back the exchange with *28. Bb3 x f7*.

27. ... Rf7 - f6
28. Be3 - g5   Qb5 - b7
There is no possible rescue. For example, after 28. ... Rf6 - g6, comes 29. d6 - d7, and the rook under attack at **c8** can't stop the d-pawn from being promoted with 29. ... Rc8 - d8, since the bishop on **g5** dominates this square.

29. Bg5 x f6   Bg7 x f6
30. d6 - d7   Rc8 - d8
The road is clear for the White queen.

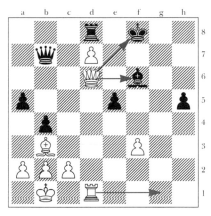

52 After 31. Qd2 - d6+: The Black king is unprotected.

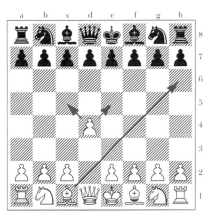

53 After 1. d2 - d4: Control of the center and development.

31. Qd2 - d6+ resigns   **52**

The checkmate is unavoidable. After 31. ... Bf6 - e7, White follows with 32. Qd6 - h6 checkmate. Also, 31. ... Kf8 - g7 and 32. Rd1 - g1+ will quickly lead to checkmate with the queen, bishop, and rook. Notice how energetically Fischer proceeded in this game. With his aggressive moves (18. h4 - h5, 21. g4 - g5, 22. Rh1 x h5, and 23. g5 - g6), he forced Larsen to defend himself in the decisive phase of the game. Black never had time to introduce his attack plan with a5 - a4. Often people who play games with castling on opposite wings will try to advance the attack as quickly as possible.

Game 5: Piece Attack Against the King

In most games, both sides will castle short. Frequently, an attack on the king is possible for one of the two parties. However, the player will not necessarily stage a pawn assault because he needs the pawns in front of his own king. The following game shows what an attack on the king with pieces can look like. Of course, the opponent must have a relatively weak point near the king which the opponent can attack. Then the attacker must bring a superior force of pieces into action to break the resistance.

**Garry Kasparov (White) –
Marjanovic (Black),
Malta, 1980**

1. d2 - d4   **53**

You've already seen games that open with 1. e2 - e4 and 1. c2 - c4. In addition to those openings, 1. d2 - d4 is a popular and good move. It frees the bishop on **c1** and occupies the center.

1. ...   Ng8 - f6

This knight move is the most popular answer to 1. d2 - d4. Black prevents 2. e2 - e4 by controlling the field with his knight. He also develops a piece and avoids the somewhat boring symmetry which follows 1. ... d7 - d5.

2. c2 - c4

White increases his control of the center, here, looking at square **d5**.

2. ...   e7 - e6

Marjanovic prepares to develop the bishop on **f8** and increases his control over **d5**.

3. Ng1 - f3   b7 - b6

You already know the concept of *fianchetto*. Black wants to use it for the bishop on **c8**. However, Kasparov is not willing to leave the h1 - a8 diagonal to the opponent without a fight. Therefore, he places his White-square bishop on the long diagonal.

4. g2 - g3   Bc8 - b7
5. Bf1 - g2   Bf8 - e7
6. 0 - 0   0 - 0   **54**

Both sides have moved their kings to safety, but they have not finished developing their pieces (especially the bishop on **c1**, the knight on **b1**, and the knight on **b8**). Nevertheless, Kasparov is already getting aggressive. He sacrifices a pawn in the center of the board to make his pieces more effective and to use a pin.

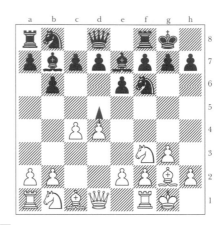

54 After 6. ... 0 - 0: Before the pawn sacrifice.

7. d4 - d5   e6 x d5
8. Nf3 - h4!

White would not gain much from 8. c4 x d5 Bb7 x d5. He would have lost a pawn without compensation. Now, on the other hand, the Black pawn on **d5** is pinned. 8. ...d5 x c4? would be avenged with 9. Bg2 x b7. In addition, the knight on **h4** can move to **f5**, where he can start an attack against the Black king.

8. ...   c7 - c6

This defends the "prey" on **d5** again, but now the bishop on **b7** is blocked out of the long diagonal until further notice. Therefore, White can capture on **d5** without the bishop being able to exchange.

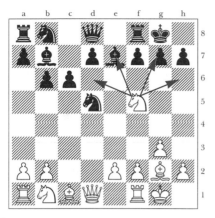

55 After 10. Nh4 - f5: The knight on f5 is ready for the attack.

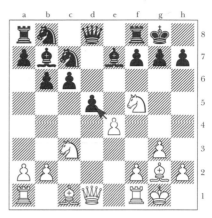

56 After 12. e2 - e4: Opening a line with a pawn exchange.

9. c4 x d5   Nf6 x d5
10. Nh4 - f5   **55**
Kasparov has brought his first attacking piece near the king.

10. ... Nd5 - c7
The knight clears **d5** so that thc Black d-pawn can occupy the center.

11. Nb1 - c3   d7 - d5
12. e2 - e4   **56**
Kasparov has sacrificed a pawn, and he wants to open the position up as fast as possible with a pawn exchange.

12. ... Be7 - f6
It would be tempting to exchange the queens with <u>12. ... d5 x e4 13. Nc3 x e4 Qd8 x d1?</u>, but the intervening move of <u>14. Nf5 x e7+</u> followed by <u>15. Rf1 x d1</u> then wins one piece.

13. e4 x d5   c6 x d5

57 After 15. Rf1 - e1: The rook occupies the e-file.

14. Bc1 - f4
Kasparov brings all his pieces to active positions.

14. ... Nb8 - a6   **57**
15. Rf1 - e1
This enhances the effectiveness of the

rook. On **e1**, it dominates a lot of important squares along the open e-file, compared to the closed f-file.

15. ... Qd8 - d7?

In this very complicated position, Marjanovic places his queen on an unlucky square. Instead, he should have moved his knight from the edge to an active square in the center, <u>15. ... Na6 - c5</u>.

16. Bg2 - h3!

White threatens to capture the Black queen with the discovered check *17. Nf5 - h6+ g7 x h6 18. Bh3 x d7*.

16. ... Kg8 - h8

Touché! Now the knight on **f5** has no square from which it can check. After <u>17. Nf5 - h6??, 17. ...Qd7 x h3</u> would follow. Because of the king's elegant side step, the knight on **f5** finds himself pinned by the queen on **d7**. But Kasparov simply brings another piece into the attack, and in the long run, the diagonal lineup Qd7 - Bh3 is not helpful for Black.

17. Nc3 - e4!

The pawn on **d5** is pinned. After <u>17. ... d5 x e4??</u> comes <u>18. Qd1 x d7</u>, capturing the queen.

17. ... Bf6 x b2

Otherwise, Kasparov would simply have played *18. Ne4 x f6 g7 x f6* on his next move, and the pawn line in front of the Black king would have

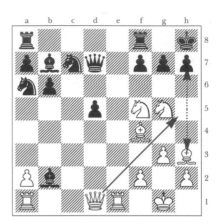

58 After 18. Ne4 - g5: On h5, the queen could control h3 and h7.

shown large holes. Black won a second pawn on **b2**, but White now starts his decisive attack against the Black king with his pieces.

18. Ne4 - g5   58

Now, the strong attack *Qd1 - h5* becomes possible. With this, White would threaten *20. Qh5 x h7 checkmate*, and also would guard the bishop on **h3** so that *20. Nf5 x g7* would threaten the queen on **d7** with the attack of the bishop on **h3**. Black no longer has a good defense.

18. ... Qd7 - c6
19. Nf5 - e7

The knight has come far. Now, he attacks the Black queen on **c6**. At the same time, he prevents Marjanovic from moving his queen to **g6**. From **g6**, she would have disturbed the attacking move, Qd1 - h5.

59 After 20 Ng5 x h7!: The decisive knight sacrifice.

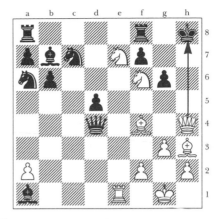

60 After 23. Nh7 - f6+: Checkmate in sight, thanks to superior pieces.

19. ... Qc6 - f6
20. Ng5 x h7!   **59**
A knight sacrifice, again with an attack on the Black queen. If Black moves 20. ...Kh8 x h7, then 21. Qd1 - h5+ Qf6 - h6(forced), and 22. Bh3 - f5+ g7 - g6 23. Qh5 x h6 checkmate.

21. ... Qf6 - d4
21. Qd1 - h5
White threatens a deadly discovered check with any move of the knight on **h7**. It would also be checkmate.

21. ... g7 - g6
Black saves himself for the moment; but after the move of the knight on **h7**, *22. ... g6 x h5* would, of course, follow.

22. Qh5 - h4
White moves his queen to a safe square and renews the threat of a discovered check with the knight on **h7**.

22. ... Bb2 x a1
The accumulation of White's pieces on the king's side no longer permits a defense.

23. Nh7 - f6+ resigns   **60**
After 23. ... Kh8 - g7 24. Qh4 - h6+ Kg7 x f6 25. Bf4 - g5 checkmate, the game is over.

Endgame Strategies

When the players exchange many pieces, and especially their queens, the game usually takes on a very special character. We call this phase of the game the endgame. Attacks are rarer because, with only a few pieces, a direct checkmate cannot be forced. In many cases, the goal is to win a pawn in order to promote it later. The kings often play an active role in the endgame, trying to increase the pressure on hostile pawns.

If rooks remain on the board in the endgame, the first side to break into the hostile position with his rooks has an advantage.

Game 6: Using the Advantage in the Endgame

In this game, former world champion Anatoly Karpov, playing White, tries to make the transition to an endgame after only a few moves. He exchanges piece after piece until he reaches a position which seems to be completely balanced. However, after Karpov's rook penetrates the seventh rank, he improves his position move by move and transforms this small endgame advantage into a final attack which brings victory.

Anatoly Karpov (White) –
Wolfgang Uhlmann (Black),
Madrid, 1973

1. e2 - e4   e7 - e6
Uhlmann uses the French Defense. The pawn on **e6** forms a bulwark against possible attacks on the c4 - f7 diagonal. At the same time, he prepares for the advance *2. ... d7 - d5* to get a foothold in the center.

2. d2 - d4   d7 - d5
3. Nb1 - d2
White has to react, because *3. ... d5 x e4* is threatened. By avoiding the exchange, <u>3. e4 x d5   e6 x d5</u>, he hopes that the Black bishop on **c8**

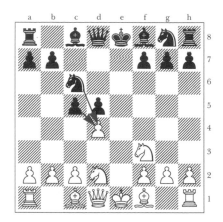

61 After 5. ...Nb8 - c6: Black applies pressure to the pawn on d4.

will have problems moving to an active position later in the game. Uhlmann, however, with his next move, creates so many possible captures in the center that a pawn exchange becomes unavoidable.

3. ...   c7 - c5
4. e4 x d5   e6 x d5
5. Ng1 - f3   Nb8 - c6   61
Black develops his knight, and pressures White's central pawn on **d4**.

6. Bf1 - b5   Bf8 - d6
7. d4 x c5   Bd6 x c5
Karpov has clarified the situation in the center. The Black pawn on **d5** no longer has a neighboring pawn and is isolated. An isolated pawn cannot be defended with his own pawns, so isolated pawns are a popular attack goal. Here, however, Karpov has a different plan. He simply wants to finalize his development and exchange some pieces

because he feels most comfortable in the endgame. He will address Black's weaknesses at that time.

8. 0 - 0   Ng8 - e7

Normally, **f6** is more suitable for the knight on **g8** than **e7**, because from **f6** he can dominate more squares. In this case, Uhlmann wants to avoid the somewhat cumbersome pin that could shortly follow 8. ... Ng8 - f6. 9. Bc1 - g5.

9. Nd2 - b3

White attacks the bishop on **c5** and clears the path for the development of the bishop on **c1**

9. ...   Bc5 - d6

The bishop is already looking at square **h2**. Black would like to start an attack on the king at a later stage of the game, but Karpov is well known for not giving his opponent an opportunity to set anything up. Therefore, he plays so that he can exchange the potentially dangerous attacker on **d6** before Black has a chance to start trouble.

10. Bc1 - g5   0 - 0
11. Bg5 - h4!   62

White prepares for *Bh4 - g3* in order to exchange material and thus nip Black's hope for an attack in the bud.

11. ...   Bc8 - g4

Here's a good move which develops the bishop and pins the knight on **f3** at the same time.

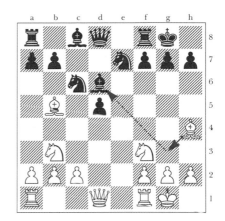

62 After 11, Bg5 -h4!: White prepares for a bishop exchange.

12. Bb5 - e2

This unchains the knight on **f3**. Karpov does not shy away from temporarily moving his pieces back for defensive purposes, as long as he can proceed with his plan for additional exchanges.

12. ...   Bg4 - h5?

Black's move isn't very useful.

13. Rf1 - e1

When nothing special is on the agenda, it is usually a good idea to place a rook on an open line, as Karpov does here.

13. ...   Qd8 - b6

This is a good move which clears **d8** for the Black rook and increases the pressure on **d4** and later on **b2**. This way, Black forces White to maneuver carefully. If, for example, White moves the knight on **b3** away,

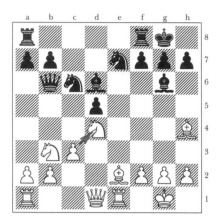

After 15. c2 - c3: Some protection for the focal point on d4.

the pawn on **b2** could be captured.

14. Nf3 - d4
"Would you exchange bishops?"

14. ... Bh5 - g6
Uhlmann knows what Karpov has in mind. Each exchange brings White closer to his goal of achieving a simplified position with attack possibilities against the isolated pawn on **d5**. Therefore, Uhlmann moves his bishop to the b1 - h7 diagonal.

15. c2 - c3
In this game, square **d4** is a focal point. White wants to protect it again.

15. ... Rf8 - e8
16. Be2 - f1
The bishop moves out of the way of the rook on **e1**.

16. ... Bg6 - e4
On **e4**, the bishop is guarding the pawn on **d5** and perhaps pressing against **g2**.

17. Bh4 - g3   Bd6 x g3
18. h2 x g3
With one pair of minor pieces gone, Karpov strives for another exchange.

18. ... a7 - a5?
This is an active move. Uhlmann would like to play 19. ... a5 - a4. If the knight on **b3** moves away, *20. ... Qb6 x b2* is possible. Nevertheless, Black gives up an important possibility with 18. ... a7 - a5. Later on, he can no longer control the sqare **b5** with a7 - a6. As always, pawn moves are binding because pawns do not have a way to turn back. The simple move, 18. ...Ra8 - d8, was best here.

19. a2 - a4   Nc6 x d4?
Presumably, Black made this play hoping to entice Karpov to 20. c3 x d4, after which Uhlmann would give good counterplay with 20. ... Ne7 - c6. However, White has a better move.

20. Nb3 x d4!   64
20. ... Ne7 - c6
After 20. ... Qb6 x b2 21. Nd4 - b5! would have followed two threats: the knight fork, *22. Nb5 - c7*, with a gain in the exchange, and *22. Re1 - e2*, which would win the queen. The Black queen simply would not have a safe square to retreat to. Apparently,

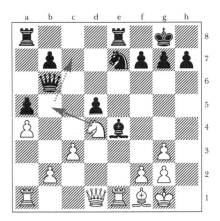

64 After 20. Nb3 x d4!: The pawn on b2 is not vulnerable because of Nd4 - b5!

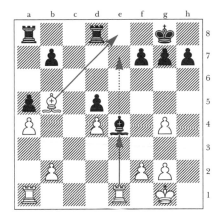

65 After 24. c3 x d4: White has the end-game advantage because of the e-file.

Uhlmann overlooked this when he moved 19. .., Nc6 x d4; otherwise he would not have played into Karpov's hands by exchanging the pieces.

21. Bf1 - b5
This is a consequence of 18. ... a7 - a5?. **b5** has become a good square for the White bishop because the Black a-pawn cannot chase him anymore. White pins the knight on **c6**.

21. ... Re8 - d8
This unpins the knight.

22. g3 - g4!
A world-champion move! The meaning becomes clear a little later. Karpov wants to deny square **f5** to the Black bishop for the rest of the game.

22. ... Nc6 x d4
Again, this is a somewhat rushed ex-

change. Black has a better move with 22. ... Ra8 - c8.

23. Qd1 x d4   Qb6 x d4
24. c3 x d4   **65**
The queens are off the board, and the endgame has arrived. At least, Uhlmann succeeded in isolating Karpov's pawn on **d4**. He must have hoped to be able to force this endgame into a draw. But Karpov's rook on **e1** is already standing on an open line. He will chase the bishop on **e4** away to create threats with his rook.

24. ... Ra8 - c8
Uhlmann also occupies an open line with a rook.

25. f2 - f3   Be4 - g6
26. Re1 - e7
The rook reaches the next-to-last rank and attacks the pawn on **b7**.

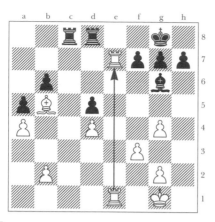

66 After 27. Ra1 - e1: Doubled rooks on the e-file.

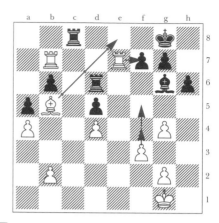

67 After 29. Re1 - e7: Doubled rooks on the seventh rank.

26. ... b7 - b6
27. Ra1 - e1   **66**
Karpov now has two rooks on the e-file. We say that he has doubled rooks. Now, if one of the Black rooks leaves the eighth rank, a checkmate can follow: 27. ... Rc8 - c2?? 28. Re7 - e8+ Rd8 x e8 29. Re1 x e8 checkmate. Uhlmann, therefore, creates some temporary breathing room for himself.

27. ... h7 - h6
28. Re7 - b7
The White rooks remain active. With 28. Re7 - b7, White attacks the pawn on **b6** and prepares for a doubling rooks on the seventh rank by clearing square **e7** for the rook on **e1**.

28. ... Rd8 - d6
29. Re1 - e7   **67**
Having two rooks on the seventh rank (for Black, on the second) creates a very strong position. Here, Karpov presses the pawn on **f7**, which is still sufficiently defended by the king and bishop. However, if White should succeed in moving his f-pawn to **f5**, then the Black king's position will quickly break down. In addition, White can increase the pressure on **f7** at any time with Bb5 - e8.

29. ... h6 - h5
The pawn on **g4** is a problem for Black. He wants to exchange him using his h-pawn. After 29. ... Rc8 - c2, 30. Rb7 - b8+ Kg8 - h7, 31. Re7 - e8 would have been possible, and the threat of *32. Re8 - h8 checkmate* would not be pleasant.

30. g4 x h5   Bg6 x h5
31. g2 - g4
Karpov does not relent. The second g-pawn is just as troublesome as the first one.

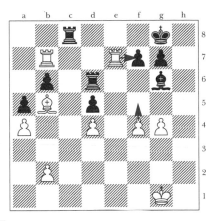

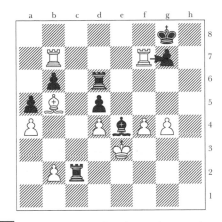

68 After 32. f3 - f4: The pawn will chase the bishop away from g6.

69 After 35. Re7 x f7: The rooks attack g7.

31. ... Bh5 - g6
32. f3 - f4
White threatens 33. f4 - f5 Bg6 - h7 34. Rc7 x f7.　　　　　　**68**

32. ... Rc8 - c1 +
The White king has little protection, but Karpov knows his opponent cannot take advantage. Black has no way to use his **d6** rook against the White king.

33. Kg1 - f2　Rc1 - c2 +
34. Kf2 - e3　Bg6 - e4
Also 34. ... Rd6 - e6+　35. Re7 x e6 d5 x e6　36. Rb7 x b6　Rc2 x b2　37. Rb6 x e6 leads to an endgame with one pawn down.

35. Re7 x f7　　　　　　　**69**
After capturing the pawn on **f7**, White wants to capture the pawn on **g7** next.

35. ... Rd6 - g6
Black defends **g7** and attacks **g4**.

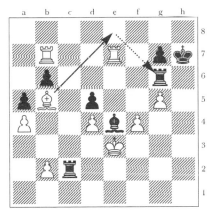

70 After 37. Rf7 - e7: The rook clears the way for Bb5 - e8 x g6.

36. g4 - g5　Kg8 - h7
Resignation. Uhlmann is powerless against Karpov's final attack.

37. Rf7 - e7　　　　　　　**70**
White prepares for *38. Bb5 - e8* because from **e8**, the bishop will attack the rook on **g6**.

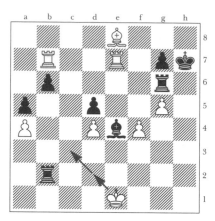

71 After 40. Ke2 - e1: The king escapes the rook's check.

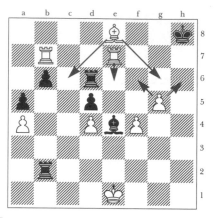

72 After 42. Rg7 - e7: The decisive attack on the king.

---

37. ... Rc2 x b2
38. Bb5 - e8
This is decisive. Black will lose the exchange on **g6** or lose his protective pawn on **g7**.

38. ... Rb2 - b3+
39. Ke3 - e2   Rb3 - b2+
40. Ke2 - e1   **71**
40. ... Rg6 - d6
More checks do not make sense, because after <u>40. ... Rb2 - b1+   41. Ke1 - d2   Rb1 - b2+   42. Kd2 - c3   Rb2 - c2+   43. Kc3 - b3</u>, the White king is safe. It is important that the rook on **g6** has no chance to take part in the attack.

41. Re7 x g7   Kh7 - h8

42. Rg7 - e7   resigns   **72**
White, with one pawn up and a decisive attack on the king, has an easy victory. The main threat is Rb7 - b8, followed by a discovered check with the bishop on **e8**.

Notice that Karpov's pieces can deny all the squares on the sixth rank to the rook on **d6**. Therefore, he cannot join in the events of the game.

You saw how Karpov's simple rook maneuvers unfolded in this game. When you reach an endgame with rooks, try to be the first one to become active on the open lines. If you succeed in penetrating the hostile camp with your rooks, as Karpov does in this game, then you'll almost automatically have a material gain.

Test 3: Final Test

The following test exercises contain strategies from the previous chapters. Therefore, unlike taking a tactics test, you are not looking to checkmate or achieve an immediate victory. Rather, you should try to find the move which does the best job of strengthening your position. Perhaps you'll activate a piece which has been passive. Maybe you'll want to increase your presence in the center, or you might want to weaken your opponent's pawn position. Don't try to look too far ahead. Find an obvious, plausible move that improves your position.

In many of the following exercises, the player is either the former world champion Capablanca or Mikhail Botvinnik. This is not a coincidence. Both of these players love to use clear strategies, which are easily illustrated. When you feel you are ready to play games that are strategically oriented, I recommend buying books of games by Botvinnik or Capablanca from a bookstore specializing in chess. As we did in the tactics tests, we provide two tips.

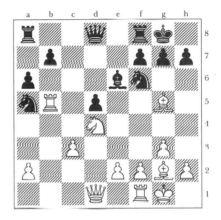

1 White's turn to move.

Black has attacked the White rook on **b5** with 1. ... a7 - a6. With his next move, White gains a lasting advantage in position.

Tip 1 With an exchange, White has access to the Black king.

Tip 2 The Black queen is pinned because she has to guard the knight on **a5**. White is able to double one of Black's pawns.

| Exercise 2 | Exercise 3 |

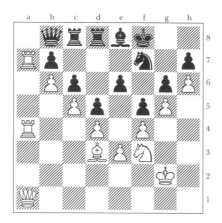

2 White's turn to move.

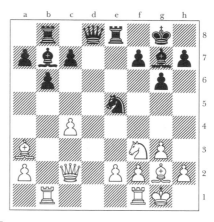

3 White's turn to move.

White directs another piece against the weakest pawn on **b7** with a maneuver requiring three moves.

Tip 1 The attacking piece is the knight.

Tip 2 The first move is 1. Nf3 - d2.

The forces are balanced. Both sides have developed their minor pieces, and both sides have already castled. Nevertheless, it is important for White to activate another piece with his next move

Tip 1 At this point, which White piece is the most ineffective?

Tip 2 White attacks the queen on **d8**.

Exercise 4	Exercise 5

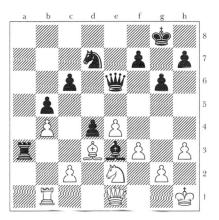

4 Black's turn to move.

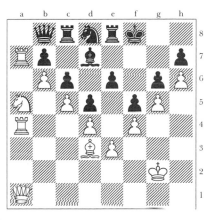

5 White's turn to move.

Black has the advantage since his bishop, rook, and queen are more active than their counterparts on the White side. What simple move increases the pressure on White?

Tip 1 The goal of the move is to prepare a sacrifice on the king's side.

Tip 2 It is a knight's move.

The position shows the game played in diagram 2 at a later stage. White has attacked the pawn on **b7** with his rook and knight. But Black can momentarily protect him with his queen and knight. How can White get material advantage?

Tip 1 The pawn on **b7** is pinned. Without him, Ra7 x d7 would be possible.

Tip 2 The bishop on **d3** is the decisive piece in the solution of this exercise.

Exercise 6	Exercise 7

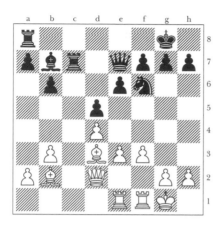

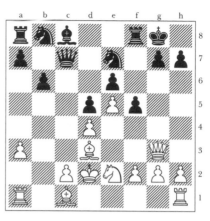

6 White's turn to move.

7 Black's turn to move.

Placing rooks on open lines is not always the correct play. Black is getting ready to double his rooks on the c-file. However, he will have no possibility of using them to invade the White camp since the squares **c1** to **c5** are secured. White, therefore, decides to forego 1. Re1 - c1, which would only lead to an exchange of all rooks. Instead, he initiates an attack in the center and later on the king's side. What is the move to do that?

Tip 1 White would like to chase away the knight on **f6** to get a chance to attack the king.

Tip 2 It is a pawn's move.

The Black position is very solid. Black has already castled, while White's king is not very safe on **d2**. Unfortunately, Black's central pawns (**d5**, **e6**, and **f5**) are standing on the same color as his bishop; and, thus, this bishop will have few opportunities to actively participate in the game. How can Black solve this problem?

Tip 1 The bishop on **d3** is essentially stronger than the bishop on **c8** since the White central pawns (**d4** and **e5**) do not hamper him.

Tip 2 If possible, Black should exchange the bishop on **c8**.

Exercise 8	Exercise 9

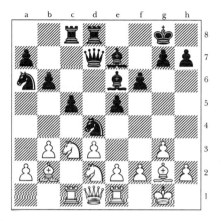

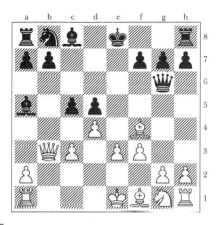

8 Black's turn to move.

9. White's turn to move.

The Black position is slightly advantageous because Black has space superiority and his knight on **d4** is in a very strong position. However, one of Black's pieces should be in an even better position. Which piece should Black move?

Tip 1 The knight on **a6** is on the edge, and he has almost no influence.

Tip 2 Black activates the knight immediately.

Finally, one last tactical exercise. White wins one piece. Be aware that 1. Qb3 - b5+ is not the solution because of 1. ... Nb8 - c6.

Tip 1 After the preliminaries, White captures with a double attack on the bishop on **a5**.

Tip 2 The queen on **b3** and the bishop on **f4** play the decisive roles in the combination attack.

117

Solutions

The Rules

In the next move, four of the White pieces can move to **d3**:

1. the pawn on **d2**:   **1. d2 - d3**
2. the bishop on **e2**:   **1. Be2 - d3**
3. the queen on **d4**:   **1. Qd4 - d3**
4. the knight on **e5**:   **1. Ne5 - d3**

The rook on **f3** cannot move to **d3** since he cannot jump over the pawn on **e3**.

In this situation, White is allowed to castle short. It does not matter that the queen on **b7** attacks his rook on h1.

However, White may not castle long here. The king would have to pass **d1**. That square is controlled by the Black rook on **d8**. In order to castle, the king may neither be in check nor pass a square on which he would be in check.

Black has five possible moves:

1. ... Kh8 - g8
1. ... a5 - a4
1. ... b4 - b3
1. ... b4 x a3
1. ... b4 x c3 *en passant*

When capturing *en passant*, Black takes the pawn on **b4** and places it on square **c3**. Black removes the pawn on **c4** from the board.

With 1. Rd1 - d8, White decides the game in his favor. The king is in check since the rook on **d8** could capture him on the next move. He cannot escape to **f8** or **h8** since the rook on **d8** could capture him there also. The White king controls **f7**, **g7**, and **h7**. Therefore, the Black king may not use those squares to flee. He has no possibility to escape the check because his bishop and rook can neither capture the rook on **d8** nor move between the rook on **d8** and the king on **g8**. Checkmate!

Between them, the two White knights have thirteen possible moves.

Nf4 - e2	**Ne5 - c4**
Nf4 - h3	**Ne5 - c6**
Nf4 - h5	**Ne5 - d7**
Nf4 - g6+	**Ne5 - f3**
Nf4 - e6	**Ne5 - g4**
Nf4 - d5	**Ne5 - g6+**
Ne5 - f7 checkmate	

The moves 1. Nf4 - g6+ and 1. Ne5 - g6+ won't produce checkmate since Black can capture the knight with 1. ... h7 x g6. After 1. Ne5 - f7, though, Black is checkmated. The king has no safe square because his own pieces block him.

Black has four ways to get out of check.

1. ... Kh8 - g7 (king flees)
1. ... Bf8 - h6 (attack line blocked)
1. ... Ra6 - h6 (attack line blocked)
1. ... Qa8 x h1 (attacker captured)

The move 1. ... Kh8 - g8 is not possible since the queen on **b3** controls **g8**. The best move for Black is 1. ... Qa8 x h1 since this move checkmates White.

Combinations

Thorez – Aljechin, Seville, 1922
1. ... Qh5 x h3! 2. g2 x h3 (The counter sacrifice 2. Qc2 x e4 fails to 2. ... Bb7 x e4 and the pawn on g2 is pinned so that Black maintains his advantage). 2. ... Ne4 - f2++ (double check!) 3. Kh1 - g1 Nf2 x h3 checkmate.

Petrosjan – Spassky, Moscow, 1966
With a sacrifice and a knight fork, White conquers the rook.

1. Qb2 - h8+!! Kg8 x h8
2. Nd6 x f7+ Kh8 - g8
3. Nf7 x g5
and White remains up by one piece and one pawn.

Tal – name unknown, Soviet Union, 1964
After 1. Be3 - b6!!, Black resigned. 1. ...a7 x b6 would be answered with 2. Qh8 - d8 checkmate. After 1. ... Qa5 x b6 2. Qh8 - h4+ Rg6 - f6 (or 2. ... f6 - f6 3. Qh4 - h7+ Rg6 - g7 4. Qh7 x g7 checkmate) would follow 3. Qh4 x b4+ (the Black queen was diverted from **a5** to **b6** and now this bishop is unguarded!) 3. ... Qb6 - d6 4. Qb4 x d6 checkmate.

Morphy – name unknown, New Orleans, 1858
The Black king has only the pawns on **g7** and **h6** for protection. With his queen, bishop, rook, and pawn, White has no trouble forcing checkmate.
1. Re7 x g7! (demolishes) Kg8 x g7
2. Qe4 x e7+ (in case of 2. Qe4 - g4+ Kg7 - h7 3. Qg4 - g6+, then 3. ... Qc6 x g6) 2. ... Kg7 - g8 3. Qe7 - f8+ Kg8 - h7 4. Qf8 - f7 checkmate.

Bareev – Kasparov, Paris, 1991
The bishop on **d4** pins the pawn on **f2**. Therefore, the beautiful move 1. ... Rb3 - g3! is possible. After that, Black threatens checkmate with 2. ... Qd5 x g2. White resigned since 2. Be2 - f3 does not save him because of 2. ... Qd5 x f3!. Although both of Black's major pieces are standing within reach of the pawns, they are not vulnerable because the pawn on **f2** is pinned by the bishop on **d4** and the pawn on **g2** by the rook on **g3**.

Final Test

Kasparov – Arlandi, Cannes, 1988
(After the moves 1. c2-c4 c7-c5 2. Ng1-f3 Nb8-c6 3. d2-d4 c5xd4 4. Nf3 x d4 Ng8-f6 5. Nb1-c3 e7-e6 6. g2-g3 Bf8-b4 7. Bf1-g2 0-0 8. 0-0 d7-d5 9.c4xd5 e6xd5 10. Bc1-g5 Bb4xc3 11. b2xc3 Bc8-e6 12. Ra1-b1 Nc6-a5 13. Rb1-b5 a7-a6.)

Kasparov recognized the chance to weaken the Black pawn position with 1. Bg5 x f6 before he brings his rook to safety. 1. ... Qd8 x f6 is not possible because of 2. Rb5 x a5. Black must answer 1. ... g7 x f6. After that, the pawns on **f7**, **f6**, and **h7** are isolated. They no longer have any neighboring pawns; and, therefore, they are weak. In the f-file, there is even an isolated doubled pawn. In addition, now the pawn on **g7** is gone. The square **h6** is not protected by a pawn any longer, and White can use it to infiltrate. Even though Black succeeded in exchanging queens relatively quickly, his king position turned out to be assailable in the endgame. The game ended:
14. Bg5xf6 g7xf6 15. Rb5-b4 Ra8-c8 16. e2-e4 d5xe4 17. Bg2xe4 f6-f5 18. Be4xf5 Be6xf5 19. Nd4xf5 8xd1 20. Rf1xd1 Rc8xc3 21. Rd1-d7 Rc3-f3 22. Rd7-d5 b7-b5 23. a2-a4 Rf3-b3 24. Rb4-g4+ Kg8-h8 25. Nf5-h6 Na5-c6 26. Rd5-f5 resigns, since he couldn't hold square f7 any longer.
After 26. ...f7 - f6, 27. Rf5 x f6! Rf8 x f6, comes 28. Rg4 - g8 checkmate. In case 26. ... Nc6 - d8, then 27. Rf5 - g5! b5 x a4 and 28. Rg5 - g8+ Rf8 x g8 29. Rg4 x g8 checkmate.

Capablanca – Treybal, Karlsbad, 1929
(After the moves 1. d2-d4 d7-d5 2.

c2-c4 c7-c6 3. Ng1-f3 e7-e6 4. Bc1-g5 Bf8-e7 5. Bg5xe7 Qd8xe7 6. Nb1-d2 f7-f5 7. e2-e3 Nb8-d7 8. Bf1-d3 Ng8-h6 9. 0-0 0-0 10. Qd1-c2 g7-g6 11. Ra1-b1 Nd7-f6 12. Nf3-e5 Nh6-f7 13. f2-f4 Bc8-d7 14. Nd2-f3 Rf8-d8 15. b2-b4 Bd7-e8 16. Rf1-c1 a7-a6 17. Qc2-f2 Nf7xe5 18. Nf3xe5 Nf6-d7 19. Ne5-f3 Rd8-c8 20. c4-c5 Nd7-f6 21. a2-a4 Nf6-g4 22. Qf2-e1 Ng4-h6 23. h2-h3 Nh6-f7 24. g2-g4 Be8-d7 25. Rc1-c2 Kg8-h8 26. Rc2-g2 Rc8-g8 27. g4-g5 Qe7-d8 28. h3-h4 Kh8-g7 29. h4-h5 Rg8-h8 30. Rg2-h2 Qd8-c7 31. Qe1-c3 Qc7-d8 32. Kg1-f2 Qd8-c7 33. Rb1-h1 Ra8-g8 34. Qc3-a1 Rg8-b8 35. Qa1-a3 Rb8-g8 36. b4-b5 a6xb5 37. h5-h6+ Kg7-f8 38. a4xb5 Kf8-e7 39. b5-b6 Qc7-b8 40. Rh1-a1 Rg8-c8 41. Qa3-b4 Rh8-d8 42. Ra1-a7 Ke7-f8 43. Rh2-h1 Bd7-e8 44. Rh1-a1 Kf8-g8 45. Ra1-a4 Kg8-f8 46. Qb4-a3 Kf8-g8 47 Kf2-g3 Be8-d7 48. Kg3-h4 Kg8-h8 49. Qa3-a1 Kh8-g8 50. Kh4-g3 Kg8-f8 51. Kg3-g2 Bd7-e8.)

White has the a-file completely under control. Because the position is so closed up, he has only a few possibilities. But Capablanca has already seen ways to increase the pressure on the Black position with a knight maneuver. He moves 1. Nf3 - d2 Be8 - d7, and Black can do nothing but wait. After 2. Nd2 - b3 Rd8 - e8 3. Nb3 - a5, he can attack the pawn on **b7** a second time.

For more about the course of this game, see Exercise 5.

Botvinnik – Smyslov, Moscow, 1958

(After the moves 1. c2-c4 Ng8-f6 2. Nb1-c3 d7-d5 3. c4xd5 Nf6xd5 4. g2-g3 g7-g6 5. Bf1-g2 Nd5xc3 6. b2xc3 Bf8-g7 7. Ra1-b1 Nb8-d7 8. c3-c4 0-0 9. Ng1-f3 Ra8-b8 10. 0-0 b7-b6 11. d2-d4 e7-e5 12. Bc1-a3 Rf8-e8 13. d4xe5 Bc8-b7 14. Qd1-c2 Nd7xc5).

With 1. Rf1 - d1, Botvinnik activates his last piece. He occupies the only completely open line of the board; and, at the same time, he attacks the Black queen. Even though the White pawn position is slightly inferior to the Black one (the pawn on **c4** has no White neighbor), the White position is slightly preferable due to the more active position of the pieces. After a long fight Botvinnik wins. Here's how:

15. Rf1-d1 Qd8-c8 16. Nf3xe5 Bb7xg2 17. Kg1xg2 Re8xe5 18. Rd1-d5 Qc8-e6 19. Rd5xe5 Bg7xe5 20. Rb1-d1 Rb8-e8 21. Qc2-e4 Be5-f6 22. Qc4xc6 Rc8xe6 23. Kg2 f3 Re6-c6 24. Rd1-c1 Bf6-d4 25. e2-e3 Bd4-c5 26. Ra3-b2 f7-f5 27. Kf3-e2 Kg8-f7 28. h2-h3 Bc5-e7 29. a2-a4 h7-h5 30. Ke2-d3 h5-h4 31. g3-g4! Rc6-c5 32. Bb2-c3 Rc5-c6 33. Rc1-g1 Rc6-d6+ 34. Kd3-c2 Be7-f6 35. g4xf5 g6xf5 36. Bc3xf6 Kf7xf6 37. Rg1-g8 Rd6-c6 38. Kc2-c3 a7-a6 39. Rg8-h8 Kf6-g5 40. Rh8-g8+ Kg5-f6 41. Rg8-h8 Kf6-g5 42. Kc3-d4 Rc6-c5 43. Rh8-h7 Kg5-g6 44. Rh7-d7! Kg6-f6 45. Rd7-d5 Rc5-c6 46. Kd4-c3 Rc6-e6 47. Rd5-d4 Kf6-g5 48.

Rd4-d7 Re6-c6 49. Kc3-b4! Kg5-f6
50. Rd7-d4! Kf6-g5 51. Rd4-d8 Rc6-
e6 52. Rd8-c8 f5-f4 53. e3xf4+
Kg5xf4 54. Rc8xc7 Kf4-f3 55. Rc7-
h7 Re6-e4 56. Rh7-h6 b6-b5 57.
a4xb5 a6xb5 58. Rh6-f6+ Kf3-g2
59. Kb4xb5 Re4-e2 60. c4-c5 Re2-
b2+ 61. Kb5-a6 Rb2-a2+ 62. Ka6-
b7 Ra2-b2+ 63. Rf6-b6 Rb2-c2 64.
c5-c6 Kg2xh3 65. c6-c7 Kh3-g2 66.
Rb6-c6 Rc2-b2+ 67. Rc6-b6 Rb2-c2
68. f2-f4 resigns

Test 3: Exercise 4

Smyslow – Botvinnik, Moscow, 1958
(After the moves 1. e2-e4 c7-c6 2.
Nb1-c3 d7-d5 3. Ng1-f3 Bc8-g4 4.
h2-h3 Bg4xf3 5. Qd1xf3 Ng8-f6 6.
d2-d3 e7-e6 7. Bf1-e2 Nb8-d7 8.
Qf3-g3 g7-g6 9. 0-0 Bf8-g7 10. Bc1-
f4 Qd8-b6 11. Ra1-b1 0-0 12. Bf4-
c7 Qb6-d4 13. Be2-f3 e6-e5 14.
Bc7-d6 Rf8-e8 15. Bd6-a3 d5xe4
16. d3xe4 b7-b5 17. Rf1-d1 Qd4-b6
18. b2-b3 Nd7-c5 19. Ba3-c1 Qb6-c7
20. Bc1-e3 Nc5-e6 21. a2-a4 a7-a6
22. b3-b4 Ra8-d8 23. Bf3-e2 Qc7-e7
24. a4xb5 a6xb5 25. Rd1xd8
Re8xd8 26. Be3-b6 Rd8-a8 27. f2-f3
Ra8-a3 28. Qg3-e1 Bg7-h6 29. Be2-
f1 Ne6-d4 30. Bb6-c5 Qe7-e6 31.
Bf1-d3 Nf6-d7 32. Bc5xd4 e5xd4
33. Nc3-e2 Bh6-e3+ 34. Kg1-h1.)

Botvinnik is in a superior position
because the White bishop on **d3** has
no move. He is standing on the same
color as the pawns **e4** and **f3**. With
1. ... Nd7 - e5!, Black increases his
advantage. He threatens 2. ... *Ne5 x*

d3 3. c2 x d3 Ra3 x d3 as well as *2. ...
Ne5 x f3! 3. g2 x d3? Qe6 x h3 checkmate.* Black is so strong that White
cannot free himself without a material
loss. Botvinnik won after a suspenseful
fight. The game continued:

34. ... Nd7 - e5 35. Qe1 - f1 Qe6 -
d6 (not immediately 35. ... Ne5 x d3
36. c2 x d3 Ra3 x d3? because of
37. Ne2 - f4! with a knight fork and
an additional attack of the queen on
f1 on the rook on **d3**).

36. f3 - f4 (otherwise White does
not have a countergame).

36. ... Ne5xd3 37. c2xd3 Ra3xd3
38. Qf1-f3 Rd3-d2 39. Rb1-f1 Qd6
xb4 40. e4-e5 Qb4-c4 41. Ne2-g3
Rd2-c2 42. f4-f5 Rc2-c1 43. e5-e6
f7xe6 44. f5xg6 Rc1xf1+ 45.
Ng3xf1 h7xg6 46. Qf3-f6 b5-b4 47.
Kh1-h2 g6-g5 48. Nf1xe3 d4xe3 49.
Qf6xg5+ Kg8-f7 50. Qg5xe3 b4-b3
51. Qe3-e5 c6-c5 52. Qe5-c7+ Kf7-
g6 53. Qc7-b8 Kg6-f5 54. Qb8-f8+
Kf5-e4 55. Qf8-f6 Qc4-d5 56. Qf6-
f3+ Ke4-d4 57. Qf3-d1+ Kd4-e5
58. Qd1-e2+ Ke5-d6 59. Qe2-a6+
Kd6-e7 60. Qa6-a7+ Ke7-f6 61.
Qa7-h7 Qd5-e5+ 62. Kh2-h1 b3-b2
resigns.

Test 3: Exercise 5

Capablanca – Treybal, Karlsbad, 1929
This is the same game as Exercise 2,
but here, the moves begin with 52.
Nf3 - d2 Be8 - d7 53. Nd2 - b3
Rd8 - e8 and 54. Nb3 - a5 Nf7 - d8.
The Black pawn on **b7** is being
attacked twice and defended twice.

With 1. Bd3 - a6!, Capablanca forced the decision. Black cannot defend the pawn on **b7** anymore. The game ended as follows:

55. Bd3-a6 b7xa6 56. Ra7xd7 Re8-e7 57. Rd7xd8+ Rc8xd8 58. Na5xc6 resigns.

Test 3: Exercise 6

Zuckertort – Blackburne, London, 1883

(Position after 1. c2-c4 e7-e6 2. e2-e3 Ng8-f6 3. Ng1-f3 b7-b6 4. Bf1-e2 Bc8-b7 5. 0-0 d7-d5 6. d2-d4 Bf8-d6 7. Nb1-c3 0-0 8. b2-b3 Nb8-d7 9. Bc1-b2 Qd8-e7 10. Nc3-b5 Nf6-e4 11. Nb5xd6 c7xd6 12. Nf3-d2 Nd7-f6 13. f2 f3 Ne4xd2 14. Qd1xd2 d5xc4 15. Be2xc4 d6-d5 16. Bc4-d3 Rf8-c8 17. Ra1-e1 Rc8-c7).

Zuckertort and Blackburne were leading players in the nineteenth century. Here, Zuckertort quickly succeeded in thrusting his pawns forward on the e-file and f-file. This opened decisive lines for his major pieces. The Black rooks in the c-line, on the other hand, do not have any effect on this game since, in the beginning, Zuckertort skillfully watches all the invasion squares. When Blackburn is able to occupy the second rank in the twenty-fifth move, the Black king has no protection and is exposed to White's combinations. The move, 1. e3-e4!, followed.

The rest of the game went like this: 18. e3-e4 Ra8-c8 19. e4-e5 (chases away the knight on **f6**) 19. ... Nf6-e8

20. f3-f4 g7-g6 21. Re1-e3 f7-f6 22. e5xf6 Ne8xf6 23. f4-f5 Nf6-e4 24. Bd3xe4 d5xe4 25. f5xg6 Rc7-c2 26. g6xh7+ Kg8-h8 27. d4 - d5+ (discovered check by the bishop on b2)

27. ... e6-e5 28. Qd2-b4 (diversion sacrifice. In case 28 ... Qe7xb4, so 29. Bb2xe5+ Kh8xh7 30. Re3-h3+ Kh7-g6 31. Rh3-g3+ Kg6-h6 32. Rf1-f6+ Kh6-h5 33. Rf6-f5+ Kh5-h6 34. Be5-f4+ Kh6-h7 35. Rf5-h5 checkmate)

28. ... Rc8-c5 29. Rf1-f8!! (Again, a diversion. After 29. ... Qe7 x f8 30. Bb2xe5+ Kh8xh7 31. Qb4xe4+ Kh7-h6 32. Rc3-h3+ Kh6-g5 33. Rh3-g3+ Kg5-h5 34. Qe4-g4+ Kh5-h6 35. Qg4-g6 checkmate.)

29. ... Kxh7 30. Qb4xe4+ Kh7-g7 31. Bb2xe5+ Kg7xf8 32. Be5-g7+!, resigns, because after 32. ... Qe7 x g7, 33. Qe4 - e8 checkmate follows.

In other moves, Black loses his queen without compensation.

Test 3: Exercise 7

Reshevsky – Botvinnik, Moscow, 1948

(Position after 1. d2-d4 e7-e6 2. e2-e4 d7-d5 3. Nb1-c3 Bf8-b4 4. e4-e5 c7-c5 5. a2-a3 Bb4xc3+ 6. b2xc3 Qd8-c7 7. Qd1-g4 f7-f5 8. Qg4-g3 c5xd4 9. c3xd4 Ng8-e7 10. Ke1-d2 0-0 11. Bf1-d3 b7-b6 12. Ng1-e2).

Black's own pawns are blocking his bishop. Often, it is a good idea to try to exchange a bishop which has no free lines. That's exactly what Botvinnik does in this game. He moves 1. ... Bc8 - a6. He isn't afraid that his underdeveloped knight on **b8** can be forced to the edge square on **a6**, because he can always move this knight again. Most important is to solve the long-lasting problem of the blocked ("bad") bishop. After the bishop exchange, Black had the better chances and could win the game after its variable course. The game continued:

12. ... Bc8-a6 13. Ne2-f4 Qc7-d7 14. Bd3xa6 Nb8xa6 15. Qg3-d3 Na6-b8 16. h2-h4 Nb8-c6 17. Rh1-h3 Ra8-c8 18. Rh3-g3 Kg8-h8 19. h4-h5 Rf8-f7 20. h5-h6 g7-g6 21. Kd2-e1 Rf7-f8 22. Nf4-e2 Nc6-b8 23. Ke1-f1 Rc8-c4 24. Kf1-g1 Nb8-c6 25. Bc1-g5 Ne7-g8 26. Ra1-e1 Qd7-f7 27. c2-c3 Nc6-a5 28. Ne2-f4 Rc4-c6 29. Bg5-f6+ Ng8xf6 30. e5xf6 Na5-c4 31. Qd3-b1 Qf7xf6 32. a3-a4 g6-g5 33. Nf4-d3 f5-f4 34. Rg3-h3 g5-g4 35. Rh3-h1 Rc6-c7 36. Qb1-d1 Qf6-g6 37. Rh1-h4 f4-f3 38. g2-g3 Rc7-f7 39. Nd3-f4 Rf7xf4 40. g3xf4 Rf8xf4 41. Qd1-b1 Rf4-f5 42. Qb1-d3 g4-g3 43. Qd3-f1 g3xf2+ 44. Kg1xf2 Rf5-g5 45. Qf1-h3 Rg5-g2+ 46. Kf2xf3 Nc4-d2+ 47. Kf3-e3 Rg2-g3+ resigns.

Kirillov – Botvinnik, Moscow, 1931
(Position after 1. c2-c4 c7-c5 2. Nb1-c3 Ng8-f6 3. g2-g3 d7-d5 4. c4xd5 Nf6xd5 5. Bf1-g2 Nd5-c7 6. Ng1-f3 Nb8-c6 7. 0-0 e7-e5 8. b2-b3 Bf8-e7 9. Bc1-b2 0-0 10. Ra1-c1 f7-f6 11. Nf3-e1 Bc8-f5 12. Nc3-a4 Nc7-a6 13.

Bb2-a3 Qd8-a5 14. Ne1-c2 Rf8-d8 15. Nc2-e3 Bf5-e6 16. d2-d3 Ra8-c8 17. Ne3-c4 Qa5-c7 18 Nc4-d2 b7-b6 19. Ba3-b2 Qc7-d7 20. Rf1-e1 Nc6-d4 21. Na4-c3).

All of Black's pieces are in good positions except the knight on **a6**. With 1. ... Na6 - b4!, Black threw this knight into the battle. If White should chase him away at some point with a2 - a3, then the pawn on **b3** becomes weak, and the knight simply withdraws to **c6** or **d5**. White's move allowed a tactical continuation: 21. ... Na6 - b4 22. Nd2 - f3 Nb4 x a2! 23. Nf3 x d4 (after 23. Nc3 x a2 comes 23. ... Be6 x b3), and the White queen has nowhere to go.

23. ... Na2xc3 24. Rc1xc3 c5xd4 25. Rc3xc8 Rd8xc8 26. e2-e3 Be7-b4 27. Re1-e2 Bb4-c3 28. e3xd4 Bc3xb2 29. Re2xb2 Qd7xd4 30. Rb2-a2 a7-a5 31. Ra2-a4 Qd4-c3 32. Ra4-h4 Qc3-c1 resigns.

Botvinnik – Sorokin, Leningrad, 1933
(Position after 1. d2-d4 Ng8-f6 2. c2-c4 e7-e6 3. Nb1-c3 Bf8-b4 4. Qd1-c2 d7-d5 5. c4xd5 e6xd5 6. Bc1-g5 Qd8-d6 7. e2-e3 Nf6-e4 8. Bg5-f4 Qd6-g6 9. Qc2-b3 c7-c5 10. f2-f3 Ne4xc3 11. b2xc3 Bb4-a5).

White wants to win the bishop on **a5** with 1. Qb3 -b5+, but the possibility 1. ... Nb8 - c6 interferes. Therefore, he plays: 1. Bf4 x b8!, resigns. After 1. ... Ra8 x b8 and 2. Qb3 - b5+ comes 3. Qb5 x a5, winning a piece.

Glossary

Battery: Two pieces, or more, supporting each other on the same rank, file, or diagonal.

Castling: Move with a rook and the king at the same time.

Castling on opposite wings: One party castles short, the other long.

Center: All-important squares in the middle of the board.

Checkmate: The goal of chess. A king is placed in check and cannot escape.

Chess opening: *See* Opening.

Combination: A forcing sequence of moves that leads to advantage.

Demolition: A sacrifice which destroys the pawn position in front of the hostile king.

Development: Moving pieces out in order to increase their effectiveness.

Diagonal battery: Queen and bishop acting together on the same diagonal.

Discovered check: Moving one's own piece so that another piece is uncovered, giving check.

Doubled pawns: Two pawns of the same color on the same file.

Doubled rooks: Rooks on the same rank or file, forming a battery.

Draw: End of game without a winner.

En passant: To immediately capture "in passing" a pawn that has just moved *two* squares from its initial square, bypassing a pawn-attacked square.

Endgame: Phase of the game in which many pieces, usually including the queens, have been exchanged.

Exchange: A sequence of moves in which a man that has captured is itself immediately captured by the opponent. Also, difference in value between a rook and a minor piece; *see* Win the Exchange.

Fianchetto: Developing a bishop on g2, b2, g7, or b7 to control one of the long diagonals (a1 - h8 or h1 - a8).

Forced mate: A sequence of moves, often with sacrifices, which checkmates an opponent's king, regardless of his moves.

Passed pawn: A pawn that cannot be blocked or captured by hostile pawns.

Gambit: Opening that includes a pawn sacrifice.

Guarding: When a pawn or piece is captured, the guarding piece can capture back.

Half-open line: File, rank, or diagonal that has no friendly pawn but does have a hostile pawn.

Invasion square: A square in the hostile camp which one's own pieces could occupy.

Isolated pawn: Pawn which has no friendly neighboring pawns.

Kingside: The half of the board including squares from the e- to the h-file.

Luft: A square in front of the king used to avoid checkmate on the eighth rank.

Major pieces: Queens and rooks.

Material: Pieces and pawns

Mating attack: Attack on the hostile king that could lead to checkmate.

Middlegame: Middle phase of the game in which the development of the pieces has been completed and the armies are in full combat.

Minor pieces: Bishops and knights.

Open line: Line in which no more pawns are standing.

Opening: First moves of the game.

Pawn duo: Two friendly pawns standing next to each other.

Pin: Holds a less valuable piece in position against the loss of a more valuable one.

Promotion: When a pawn reaches the last rank, it becomes a piece of the player's choice, except another king. The pawn often "queens."

Queenside: The half of the board including squares from the d- to the a-file.

Sacrifice: A sequence of moves in which a player gives up material in order to achieve other advantages.

Shepherd's mate: Checkmate in four moves with the queen and bishop (also known as Scholar's mate).

Stalemate: Draw, since one player has no more possible moves but is not in check.

Starting rank: For White, the first rank; for Black, the eighth rank.

Win the Exchange: To gain a rook against the loss of a knight or a bishop.

Zugzwang: A position in which every possible move worsens one's own position.

Zwischenzug: An "in-between" move.

Index
(Masters, Games, and Tests)

About the Author

ENNO HEYKEN, an international chessmaster and trainer of the German Chess Association, wrote his thesis about the psychology of chess. He is currently a certified psychologist with a practice in job-finding, and teaches chess as an adult college course.